THE PRAYER OF THE FAITHFUL

Understanding and Creatively Using the Prayer of the Church

by Walter C. Huffman

Augsburg Publishing House
Minneapolis, Minnesota

Acknowledgments

Material from the following sources is acknowledged: Forms A and J: *Lutheran Book of Worship*, copyright © 1978. Form B: *Lutheran Book of Worship: Ministers Desk Edition*, copyright © 1978. Form C: *We Pray to the Lord*, copyright © 1984 Ave Maria Press. Forms D, E, F, G, H, and I: *Book of Common Prayer*, copyright © 1979 by Charles Mortimer Guilbert as custodian. Form K: *Praise God: Common Prayer at Taize*, copyright © 1977 Oxford University Press. Form L: Hymn stanzas from "When in Our Music God Is Glorified" by F. Pratt Green. Copyright © by Hope Publishing Company, Carol Stream IL 60188. All rights reserved. Used by permission. Arrangement in *The Wideness of God's Mercy*, copyright © 1985 The Seabury Press. Form M: *Come, Lord Jesus*, copyright © 1976, 1981, Lucien Deiss. All rights reserved. Published by World Library Publications. Form N: Copyright © 1970 The Liturgical Conference, 806 Rhode Island Ave. NE, Washington, DC 20018. All rights reserved. Used by permission.

ISBN 0-8066-2230-X

Avis Benson, cover design

Prepared under the auspices of
the Division for Life and Mission in the Congregation
and the Board of Publication of the American Lutheran Church

Contents

Introduction

Thomas Merton was a fully contemporary man who dared to commit himself to a lifelong search for an authentic way of life. This singular passion led him to combine in one rich life a unique variety of roles—prolific spiritual writer and poet, hermit and social activist—all while living at a Trappist monastery in Kentucky. For a secluded monk under a vow of silence, Merton has had considerable influence on our search for an appropriate Christian style of spirituality and prayer.

In spite of his expertise in this area, he advised great humility concerning the life of prayer.

One cannot begin to face the real difficulties of prayer and meditation unless one is first perfectly content to be a beginner and really experience oneself as one who knows little or nothing, and has a desperate need to learn the bare rudiments. Those who think they "know" from the beginning will never, in fact, come to know anything.

We do not want to be beginners. But let us be convinced of the fact that we will never be anything but beginners all our life.[1]

Many committed Christians are frustrated by their inability to pray. A sea of pressures and preoccupations threaten to obliterate communion with God. The wide range of publications on prayer and spirituality witness to the search for an answer to what Dietrich Bonhoeffer called the "agony of prayerlessness." To be a beginner, according to Merton, is to know again the need to reach out for help to God and to others for spiritual formation. This book is written for such beginners who wish to explore the implications of intercessory prayer and its meaning for public worship, congregational life, and individual prayer.

The contemporary liturgical movement has devoted great energy to understanding eucharistic prayer and its function in the Sunday assembly. The fruits of these labors speak for themselves in the emerging consensus on language, content, and style of the Great Thanksgiving. On the other hand, comparatively little attention has been given to the ancient prayer of the faithful, the role of intercessor, and the impact of intercession on Christian spirituality. The recent renewal of liturgy in mainline denominations has pointed to the importance of this intercessory element, but little assistance has been offered to enrich its expression. If the prayer of the faithful is to be a positive force in worship, then there needs to be skilled and well-informed leadership as well as greater understanding by the community itself. This seems to be a good time to raise up this ministry of intercession as a sign of care for others and the world.

In early Christian worship, immediately following the departure of the uninitiated, a deacon led the so-called prayer of the faithful. As a "blue-collar cleric," the deacon's work in the community among the faithful and poor provided a deep link with the daily life of the people. This solidarity of people and prayer, liturgy and life, made a deacon the appropriate agent of intercession in the life of the church. The renewal of such an office means that we must understand not only its charitable and pastoral dimensions, but also its liturgical expression: the prayer of the faithful.

In different periods and different traditions, there have been terminological shifts in what history has designated the prayer of the faithful. Because of the historical component in this book, this term (which is still common to the Roman Catholic Church) has been retained. There are, however, other appropriate terms that are employed when the context seems to invite their usage. The eucharistic liturgy of *Lutheran Book of Worship*[2] refers to this phenomenon in its rite as the Prayers while in another section of the book an example is entitled the Prayer of the Church. Although this term—the Prayer of the Church—has been used as a generic term for the entire liturgy, it is worthy because it recalls ecclesial and liturgical themes that are essential to its definition. The Episcopal *Book of Common Prayer*[3] has settled on the term Prayer of the People, while other Protestants pick up this intercessory theme in what is variously called Pastoral Prayer, General Prayer, Universal Prayer, Intercessions, or some similar term.

In books that deal with liturgical themes, those that show their scholarship are usually aimed at pastors, teachers, and seminarians while the "nuts and bolts" manuals are reserved for "the average layperson." The result has sometimes been an uninformed performance of assigned tasks in liturgical ministries. This book seeks to provide an exegetical and historical basis for a ministry of intercession as well as providing chapters that encourage creative practice. It is written for the broad audience of those who will be drawn into such an endeavor.

It would be profitable for those involved in the ministry of intercession to gather for a brief course on prayer. This book, along with other selected works, could serve as texts for such a course. Further discussion of this concept is included in Chapter 4.

Like a road map which amplifies a certain metropolitan area because of its importance, so the first two chapters of this book focus on key biblical themes rather than attempting an extensive survey of intercession in Old and New Testament. Chapter 1 uses the Psalms, staple for a biblically-founded spirituality, to point to the doxological nature of prayer–speech in the Judeo-Christian tradition. The second chapter studies the New Testament catechesis on prayer and focuses on its center-piece, the Lord's Prayer. In Chapter 3, the practice of formal intercessory prayer in public worship is traced from its origins in the early church to the present day.

These biblical and historical studies prompt practical ideas and guidelines for the shaping of intercessory prayer. The final two chapters seek to collect and to expand upon these insights in exploring the role of those who are called to be intercessors in our communities. The nature of intercession and its expression through the preparation and presentation of the prayer leader is explored in Chapter 4. A collection of intercessory prayers included in the Appendix are used in Chapter 5 as texts for a running commentary on content, form, and language.

In a germinal form, I "began" this and other liturgical projects as a seminary student under Eugene L. Brand. My experience as the pastor of Christ the King

Lutheran Church in Richmond, Virginia, and now, almost a decade of teaching and leading worship at Trinity Lutheran Seminary in Columbus, Ohio, have been the substantive sources of study and practice. A recent sabbatical experience at Upper Arlington Lutheran Church provided important opportunity for exploring this theme in worship and educational forums.

Special thanks to Buff Delcamp, a collaborator at Upper Arlington, and Dolly Katz and Phyllis Dawson who typed the manuscript.

Chapter 1

Praisemaking: Prayer in a Doxological Key

It is indeed right and salutary that we should at all times and in all places offer thanks and praise to you, O Lord, holy Father, through Christ our Lord.[1]

One of the earliest accounts of Christian worship is the correspondence between Pliny the Younger, governor of the Roman provinces of Bithynia and Pontus, and the Roman emperor Trajan. In a bureaucratic exchange from the year A.D. 112, Pliny reports his dealings with a secret religious sect and asks the emperor's advice. From interrogating some renegade members of this group he seems to conclude that they pose no great threat to the status quo since "the sum of their guilt . . . amounted only to this, that on an appointed day they had been accustomed to meet before daybreak, and to recite a hymn antiphonally to Christ, as to a god." He goes on to add information about their oath to live upright lives and that they eat a meal of "ordinary and harmless food."[2]

The biblical witness gives strong support to Pliny's description of the early church as a community engaged in praise. In a few key lines, the author of Acts summarizes the life of the community where "day by day, attending the temple together and breaking bread in their homes, they partook of food with glad and generous hearts, praising God and having favor with all the people" (Acts 2:46-47). Paul's call to the Colossians to let the word of Christ come alive in "psalms and hymns and spiritual songs" is backed up by his own tendency to frame and punctuate letters with doxological statements. From Luke's canticles celebrating the birth of Christ to the final hallelujah chorus of the Apocalypse, we are impressed with the priority of praise in the life of the early church.

There exists graphic evidence of this doxological tendency. In the childlike strokes on the tufa stone of the catacombs and in the sepulchral art of the sarcophagi, we meet the central characters of stories that shaped the church's understanding of its faith, life, and mission: Three young men stand in the fiery furnace singing, "All you works of the Lord, bless the Lord." Noah is on the bow of a tomblike ark sailing through the flood. Moses stands by the rock; Lazarus springs from the tomb. We see "spirit portraits" of beloved relatives. These saints often have a common physical characteristic: their bodies are praise shaped! Called *orants*, their arms and hands are raised in a sign of blessing and praise. Such a posture is not only a prayer–praise pose, but it also reveals a doxological style of living and dying.

Praise is the church's highest calling. At the heart of the Christian faith is the joyful recognition:

Blessed be the God and Father
of our Lord Jesus Christ!
In great mercy

he has given us
the rebirth of a living hope
through the resurrection of
Jesus Christ from the dead,

An incorruptible inheritance
undefiled and unfading
kept in heaven for you
guarded by God's power
through faith
for revelation
in the last time (1 Peter 1:3-5).[3]

It is only natural to express this mystery in the passionate language of vision and hymn and poetry. Doxology, the language of praise, is our native tongue. At a distance behind this doxological mode lives the more reasoned language of theology which reflects, corrects, and refines what was originally said in praise-speech. Doxology and theology, therefore, form the yin and yang of Christian expression—a complement of left brain/right brain thinking and imaging. Despite their essential closeness, it is clear that praise is still our first business and deserves our most concerted attention.

In his sermon on the ten lepers, Luther emphasizes the priority of praise:

True worship is to turn back and with a loud voice glorify the Lord. This is the greatest work in heaven and on earth, indeed the only one that we may give to God, for he needs no other and accepts nothing from us but love and praise.[4]

Intercessors, those who pray for others, must rediscover this primary importance of praise. Praise provides the context for our petitions and prayers. Praise precipitates mission and provides a rationale for our missionary impulse as advocate and servant. In praise we experience something of the final age to come and thereby find power and hope in our present day.

The Psalms as Primer

A primer is a book that covers the basics of a given subject. A primer is the necessary undercoat of paint that insures a successful finished product. A primer is a device used to detonate explosives. The Psalms are primers in all of the above senses—schooling us in the basics, laying foundations, and activating our ministry of intercession and prayer.

The book of Psalms provides the most reliable theological, pastoral, and liturgical resource given us in the biblical tradition. In season and out of season, generation after generation, faithful women and men turn to the Psalms as a most helpful resource for conversation with God about the things that matter most.[5]

Throughout Christian history, the Psalter has been the staple of a biblically-based spirituality. Revealing the church's high regard for this prayerbook of the Bible, references to and verses from psalmic material are generously strewn throughout the pages of the New Testament. Monastic communities often disciplined themselves to pray the "entire David" during a week of daily prayer offices. Calvin and the

Reformed tradition felt that only the Psalms should be the songs of Christian worship. Luther loved the Psalms and thought that whoever begins to pray the Psalter seriously and regularly would soon give a vacation to other little devotional prayers saying "Ah, there is not the juice, the strength, the passion, the fire which I find in the Psalter."

In the church today, there is a certain ambivalence in the use of the Psalms. While we may hear the urging of scholars and worship leaders to rediscover this treasure, we simply are not convinced that the effort is worth it. They are used only occasionally in public worship and in the individual Christian's prayer life. The problem is one of distance between our modern high-tech society, and an environment and life so remote from our own. Words, images, poetic forms, the lament genre that complains and rails against God seem alien to our present experience. And so we equivocate, affirming the Psalms as somehow vital because of their importance in Scripture, but finding little use for them in our lives.

It is the premise of this chapter that certain characteristics of psalms that disenchant people today are characteristics that are most profound in shaping the prayer of the church and our spirituality.

The "Givenness" of Psalmody

One area of spiritual sickness today is a narcissism that seeks out and appropriates that which best suits me: I attend a congregation "where my needs are met" and where I can associate with like-minded people. In sermon, small group study, and private reading, I listen and read in a selective fashion using God's Word as prescription for some perceived sickness. A raging personalism measures everything by *my* opinion of what is most useful to *me*.

An ancient approach to praying the Psalms is to pray them in a given order, fitting oneself into a biblical or liturgical pattern rather than forcing the Psalms into our own. Instead of asking what they have to do with us we must ask what we have to do with them and what we hear of God's will through them. In *Psalms: Prayerbook of the Bible,* Dietrich Bonhoeffer writes:

It does not depend, therefore, whether the Psalms express adequately that which we feel at a given moment in our heart. If we are to pray aright, perhaps it is quite necessary that we pray contrary to our own heart. Not what we want to pray is important, but what God wants us to pray. . . . The richness of the Word of God ought to determine our prayer, not the poverty of our heart.[6]

To pray what may be "contrary to the heart" is to sacrifice a purely self-interested approach to Christian prayer. This moving beyond oneself enables us to stand in the stream of prayer-praise history of the people of God and to share in their images and insights.

To be honest, to be valid, many feel that prayer must surge from the heart in a stream of original sentences or stammerings. While there will always be the prayer of the heart and one's inarticulate reaching toward God, there must come again emphasis on the "givenness" of biblical praise-speech so characteristic of the Psalter.

No language, however eloquent or nuanced, could capture or define the specific quality of any moment. Even under intense emotion, I do not seek for some novel mode of expression. It would be like writing all new Christmas carols every year, or like searching for alternatives, having decided that the phrase "I love you" has grown hackneyed. I return gratefully to the simple, familiar, general, allusive terms that I and thousands of others have used before.[7]

The Relevance of Ancient Categories

Another roadblock to our appreciation of the Psalms is their archaic nature. What have burnt offerings and firmaments to do with computers and space shuttles? There are centuries of difference between the praisemakers of ancient Israel and contemporary Christians. The chasm yawns between life-styles, world views, and environments. For many, this great distance turns the Psalter into a kind of "spiritual heirloom" tucked away in some hope chest but quite useless in everyday life.

Contradicting this initial view is the persistent use of psalms and hymns *in spite of* their archaic language. Most of those people who pray, "The Lord is my shepherd," have never seen a shepherd and know nothing about the care of sheep or the particulars of such a pastoral vocation. Nevertheless they fervently pray this psalm and experience the power of its meaning for their lives.

Anthropologists who study ritual and myth believe that "archaic" is not a bad but a good word. The Greek root *arche* has the double meaning of "rule" and "beginning" and it hints at themes of authority and sacred origins. In other words, it is in the very nature of religious ritual language to use archaic forms that put us in touch with our foundations in God's creative purpose. In this case, linguistic distance gives the psalms a validity for every age.

This insight of behavioral sciences into the power of the archaic in ritual language explains some of the continuing appeal of a King James Version or a Latin mass despite proliferating biblical translations and new liturgies. Our passion to contemporize religious rites and words may be a misplaced fervor if in so doing we unmask the archaic aura of great words.

A regular praying of the Psalms teaches us surprising lessons about the language of prayer and praise. Words and images that are used for centuries in public worship have layers of meaning that are often rich and durable. They possess an ability to communicate the traditions of the faith with fresh authority. While vernacular translations of Scripture and "folk liturgies" preserve us from obscurity and ignorance, the very immediacy of understanding some words causes us to treat them casually and superficially. The psalms invite us to savor word-thoughts and to penetrate into the deeper realities of the faith.

At the center of this phenomenon of ancient categories is the simple and profound need to "remember the works of the Lord and call to mind the wonders of old time" (Psalm 77:11). In his book, *The Psalms*, Claus Westermann says that "only those who praise do not forget." The genius of praise is this motif of powerful remembering. On the other hand, turning away from God happens whenever praise is silenced.

In the Psalms, the Hebrew poets delight in cataloging the mighty acts of God. They rehearse their experiences of one who "heals all our diseases . . . saves from

10

destruction . . . withholds no good thing . . . fills our life with goodness . . . provides for all our needs . . . gives bread to the hungry . . . peace to the troubled." In such memories we find faith articulated and offered to all generations. With the psalmist, we come to the conclusion: "This is the way God, our God acts! Praise the Lord!"

Seasons of the Spirit

Our lives move through seasons of birth and death, sickness and recovery, laughter and weeping, light and darkness. The Psalms embrace these polarities of human existence, showing us a path and offering us a faith interpretation for the journey.

In a recent work on the Psalms, Walter Brueggemann suggests that the pattern of these seasons is a pattern of orientation, disorientation, and new orientation. While he does not want to straitjacket the Psalms in any one neat grid, he offers this paradigm as a helpful and convincing way in which the Psalms interface with our human experience.[8]

During the seasons of orientation, things fit together and life makes sense. At such times it is easy to trust God and to sing,

I will exalt you, O God my king,

and bless your name

forever and ever (Psalm 145:1).

Discontinuity comes when we experience personal or public crises—illness, shame, joblessness, inhumanity, war, death—and life is filled with questions and despair. In psalms of lament we dare to cry,

How long, O Lord?

Will you forget me forever?

How long will you hide your face from me? (Psalm 13:1).

And then there are the blessed times of new orientation when, just when we thought our world had ended, a new coherence comes to us. Such moments of new life are inexplicable. They surprise us while we are "in the pits." During such times there is an overwhelming sense of resolution and thanksgiving in which we long for "a thousand tongues"—we are "lost in wonder, love, and praise."

You have turned my wailing into dancing;

you have put off my sackcloth

and clothed me with joy.

Therefore my heart sings to you

without ceasing;

O Lord my God,

I will give you thanks forever (Psalm 30:12-13).

In this process, the psalms of lament—which recognized times of negativity and dare to blame God for this disorientation—deserve special attention. Those psalms storm heaven with angry complaints. They celebrate the potential ruin of enemies. They reveal an earthy, honest faith. As such they are an affront to the usual piety of our day which strives to be superficially polite and always positive in prayer.

As children of the Enlightenment, we have censored and selected around the voice of darkness and disorientation, seeking to go from strength to strength,

11

from victory to victory. But such a way not only ignores the Psalms; it is a lie in terms of our experience. . . . The Psalms are a boundary thrown up against self-deception. They do not permit us to ignore and deny the darkness, personally or publicly, for that is where new life is given.[9]

There is profound health in a spirituality that can give voice to negative as well as positive evidence. Psalms of lament invite praise not only "because of" the situation but "in spite of" the circumstances. Therapeutically they help us bring that which is dark and angry into the light where it can be seen and processed. Such psalms warn against an easy spirituality that would avoid the hard questions of pain, injustice, and suffering in our lives and in our world. They challenge us to a radically honest life of prayer with the one who is Lord of all.

The Liturgical Shaping of the Psalms

The Psalms originated in the circumstances of everyday life. Born in harvest fields and battlefields, sickbeds and marketplaces, they arose out of the great commonality of human experience. Like the Negro spiritual, their authors are unknown. Later editors would affix superscriptions to certain psalms as a way of relating them to individuals (A Psalm of David) or events ("when Nathan the prophet came to him"), but these were pious intentions stressing the deep connection of the psalm with salvation history. Indeed we should probably speak of anonymous authors because the long process of oral transmission meant that generations of people collaborated in their formation. These characteristics—circumstantiality, anonymity, collaboration—give the Psalms an unusual capacity to be the prayers and song of people in every generation.

The primary home and final destination of these psalms was the worshiping assembly. Scholars even refer to some psalms as liturgies because of their obvious connection with pilgrimages, blessings, the eating of sacred meals, or the performance of a sacrifice. All psalms, even those labeled individual psalms of lament or praise, were finally shaped by the corporate worship life of Israel. Long before they became the written material of private devotions, they were the sung prayers of public worship.

This social motif is inherent in the poetic nature of the Psalms. The rhyme is one of meaning and thought rather than sound or number of syllables and is often expressed in some form of parallel structure. This pattern reveals the nature of performance where choir, choir leader, and people antiphonally sing and listen, rehearsing with each other the repertoire of their faith and life. In *Life Together*, Dietrich Bonhoeffer speaks of this social and public character:

> The psalms teach us to pray as a fellowship. The body of Christ is praying, and as an individual one acknowledges that his prayer is only a minute fragment of the whole prayer of the church. He learns to pray the prayer of the body of Christ. And that lifts him above his personal concerns and allows him to pray selflessly.[10]

As liturgical text, we are confronted by the uniqueness of the Psalms as sung prayers or prayed songs. Saturated with metaphor and symbol, they grab at the ecstatic roots of all human discourse. As such, they reach for words beyond words, calling attention to their own limits, and thus, implicitly pointing to the one who has no limits. Lyrical and humane, the Psalms do not seek to impress but to glorify God. Such prayer is language doing what it does best—recognizing its own limits and pointing to the one who is limitless.

In the Psalms we often hear a disembodied voice calling us to praise: "O magnify the Lord with me." "Come, let us praise." Sometimes it is an inward shout: "Bless the Lord, O my soul, and all that is within me bless his holy name." Sometimes this voice calls on all creation to "Praise him, sun and moon . . . stars . . . waters . . . wild beasts . . . sea monsters. . . ." To obey this call is to be drawn into the Jewish tradition of thanksgiving which dominates prayer in congregational, familial, and personal contexts. We move into biblical patterns of prayer that stretch parochial categories, teaching us that prayer in the assembly is prayer par excellence. The usual stereotypes about language are challenged as we find surprising relevance in archaic forms and discover the possibilities of prayer as song. To turn and praise God in all the seasons of our lives is to give God our ultimate allegiance. It is to undermine the political and economic realities of our day that demand our loyalty and to experience something of the liberation that is ours in Jesus Christ.

Chapter 2

Our Father:
The Prayer That Forms Us

He was praying in a certain place, and when he ceased, one of his disciples said to him, "Lord, teach us to pray, as John taught his disciples" (Luke 11:1).

In certain geographical centers the early church reserved the privilege of praying the "Our Father"[1] for full members of the community—those who had been through the rigors of pre-baptismal training and had entered into the mysteries of the faith at the Vigil of Easter. Near the time of their Baptism, they were taught the meaning of this prayer of believers and after their first communion these new members of the church were allowed to pray it aloud with other Christians as a public sign of their new status in the community. Their unity with Christ and his purposes was prerequisite to praying their Lord's Prayer and, at the same time, the praying of this prayer shaped their lives in him.

Those first believers would be shocked at our present use of the "Our Father." This sacred treasure is often used as an empty device to open or close meetings or as a team prayer before a school athletic event. Believers and nonbelievers alike mouth the words as a casual sign of their religiosity. Even committed Christians are hard pressed to explain the meaning of the petitions they have prayed for years.

These problems of ignorance and irrelevance are not new. Martin Luther once wrote: "The Lord's Prayer is the greatest martyr, for everybody tortures and abuses it." Familiarity breeds contempt, we say, but like a marriage that flourishes and grows over the years, familiarity can also breed greater love. So Luther also spoke of this prayer with great reverence saying, "There is no nobler prayer to be found on earth, for it has the excellent testimony that God loves to hear it. Thus we should not trade it for all the riches in the world."

In our speechlessness before God, Jesus invites us to pray with him. The beauty of scriptural prayer is that it is simultaneously the Word of God and our word. In the Psalms something wonderful has been made known, and the praise-makers of Israel respond in a lyrical telling to God what God has already revealed. The Word of God becomes the material of human doxology as Creator and creature, Redeemer and redeemed become one in this unique medium. Even more wonderful is the New Testament claim that Jesus gives a prayer that supercedes all other forms of communication with God. This is pure grace, writes Bonhoeffer, that God tells us how we can speak with God and have fellowship with God.

The child learns to speak because his father speaks to him. He learns the speech of his father. So we learn to speak to God because God has spoken to us and speaks to us. Repeating God's own words after him we begin to pray to him.[2]

When we pray "through Jesus Christ our Lord" as we do in the ancient collects, we give voice to this vital companionship of Christ with us in prayer. All Christian prayer is informed and formed by the prayer of Jesus which becomes the New Testament's centerpiece for its teaching on prayer.

Learning to Pray after Jesus

Both Luke 11:1-13 and Matthew 6:5-15 have collected and preserved what amounts to an early Christian catechesis on prayer. From the standpoint of the liturgical life of the church, these texts recall material used to initiate the newly baptized into the mysteries of the faith. Variations in the accounts are due to differing traditions and audiences. In each, however, the Lord's Prayer is the foundational centerpiece.

Luke begins his catechesis on prayer by showing us Jesus, "praying in a certain place." This pointing to Jesus before reporting his words about prayer or even the words of the "Our Father" itself signal that all Christian prayer derives its power and purpose through Jesus. In his life, death, and resurrection he embodies the prayer he teaches his disciples. As a summary of his gospel, this prayer belongs to him; it is the *Lord's* Prayer. When the disciples press him to teach them to pray "as John taught his disciples," they remember prayer as a characterization of the one who prays and as identifying mark between teacher and disciples. Such prayer is not a collection of pious words but a way of being before God and of being with those for whom we pray.

After this opening picture of Jesus as prototype for all Christian prayer, Luke stresses the necessity of persistence in prayer.

And he said to them, "Which of you who has a friend will go to him at midnight and say to him, 'Friend lend me three loaves; for a friend of mine has arrived on a journey, and I have nothing to set before him', and he will answer from within, 'Do not bother me; the door is now shut, and my children are with me in bed; I cannot get up and give you anything'?" (Luke 11:5-7).

The parable is one long rhetorical question, asking that which has an obvious and expected answer. Would you go to a friend at night when you are in need? Well, yes, if that person was *indeed* a friend. And can you imagine such a friend telling you to go away because he or she has put out the cat and has locked the door? In spite of the problems of getting up and tripping over the sleeping children, can you imagine that your friend would not observe the almost sacred responsibility to be hospitable? No, of course not! That would be unthinkable! But for the sake of argument, let us imagine that this "friend" was out of sorts and did give such an answer.

I tell you, though he will not get up and give him anything because he is his friend, yet because of his importunity he will rise and give him whatever he needs (Luke 11:8).

Persistence is one sure way to bother this sleeper awake and get the needed bread for the midnight traveler. The word *importunity* in this translation means "a dogged and troublesome demanding of something." Like the widow harranging the judge into submission (Luke 18:2-8), Luke encourages a kind of spiritual tenacity to "always pray and not lose heart" (Luke 18:1).

The early church took this advice seriously as it adopted rigorous patterns of

15

communal daily prayer. One of the first manuals on the life and worship of the Christian community, the *Didache,* in discussing the "Our Father," instructs the faithful to "pray thus three times a day."[3]

Some commentators believe that in the parable of the midnight visitor, the original emphasis was on the friend who is importuned rather than on the one who does the persistent knocking at midnight. Even if the friend grumbles at the idea of getting up in the middle of the night, the shame of being inhospitable is more than sufficient to move him. The interpretation was this: If the importuned has to answer a friend because of this sense of duty, how much more must God hear you!

So this important parable on prayer not only urges unwearied asking, but it also reveals the gospel promise of God's steadfast love. Jesus assures his own, "Ask, and it will be given you; seek, and you will find; knock, and it will be opened to you." Arguing from the lesser human context to the greater expectation of God, Jesus promises, "How much more will the heavenly Father give. . . ."

And then we encounter a surprise ending to this section on prayer. While we have been dealing with parables and pictures that involve loaves of bread, fish, eggs—"good gifts"—Jesus now concludes,

If you then, who are evil know how to give good gifts to your children, how much more will the heavenly Father give the Holy Spirit to those who ask" (Luke 11:13).

In the final analysis, it is not what God can give us, but rather it is God himself that we need! The answer to Christian prayer is not a cornucopia of things or even the magic of changed circumstances, but rather God himself.

In Matthew's account, Jesus strongly rejects the standing model of piety practiced in the Pharisaic circles of his day. Matthew's audience would have been familiar with those Jesus called "hypocrites . . . in the synagogues and in the streets" whose approach to almsgiving, prayer, and fasting was characterized by a vain craving of public approval. Over and over in this account he contrasts their behavior with the injunction "but when you . . ." and supplies examples of right conduct. His teaching reveals an emphatic concern for the inner disposition of those who pray.

Jesus spoke to the perennial problem of confusing fine words and pious sounds with true prayer. To counter the tendency to "heap up empty phrases" as a way of winning favor with God and with others, Jesus offers the "Our Father" as an example of brief prayer. Behind the slightly different versions of this prayer in Matthew and Luke lies an original prototype that was astoundingly concise. It is suggested that the oldest wording resembles the following:

Father (Abba)

Hallowed be your name,

Your kingdom come,

The bread of tomorrow give us today,

Forgive us our sins,

  and we forgive those

    who sin against us,

Save us from the time of trial.[4]

Our usual praying of the Lord's Prayer has been based on the longer version in

Matthew which, with its expansions and parallelism in certain lines, reflects its early use in the liturgy of the church. The theoretical "original" above clearly sets forth the essential themes of the prayer. Those themes will be explored in the rest of this chapter.

The Words God Loves to Hear

Abba: Naming God

We are beneficiaries of a century of massive research into the nature and meaning of scriptural texts carried on by such scholars as Joachim Jeremias, the late professor of New Testament studies at Gottingen University in Germany. With his students he mounted a massive survey of the Old Testament, rabbinic writings, and the literature of surrounding cultures in an effort to determine the significance of one word. That word is the first word of the Lukan account of the Lord's prayer, *abba,* the Aramaic equivalent of the word "father."

Jeremias discovered the occasional use of the generic "father" as name for God in some Oriental literature. This was an inclusive term indicating qualities of paternal authority as well as characteristics such as tenderness associated with motherhood. The naming of God as Father in the Old Testament occurs in the prophets where God in great mercy forgives Ephraim, his "firstborn" (Jeremiah 31:9), his "dear son," his "darling child" (Jeremiah 31:20). In these passages we encounter a prodigal love that surpasses our human experience.

Only in the New Testament, however, do we find the homey, family word, *abba,* used to address God as father. *Abba* is a child's word associated with the first babbling sounds of an infant. It means something close to "dear father." Speaking of the uniqueness of this term in such a context, Jeremias writes:

> No Jew would have dared to address God in this manner. Jesus always . . . spoke with God as a child speaks with his father, simply, intimately, securely, childlike in manner. . . . In this term *abba* the ultimate mystery of his mission and authority is expressed. . . . This term *abba* is the *ipsissima vox* ("actual way of speaking") of Jesus and contains *in nuce* ("in a nutshell") his message and his claim to have been sent from the Father.[5]

In the Gospels, Jesus addresses God using the term *abba* no less than 170 times. In the Lord's Prayer Jesus allows his disciples a share in his sonship by authorizing them to repeat the word *abba* after him. Paul makes this abundantly clear when he writes:

> When we cry *"Abba!* Father!" it is the Spirit himself bearing witness with our spirit that we are children of God, and if children, then heirs, heirs of God and fellow heirs with Christ (Romans 8:15b-17).

It is hard to overemphasize the significance of this little word *abba*. Like *amen* and *alleluia* it was carried over into the liturgical prayer of some communities even though the remainder of their prayer was in another language. From very ancient times, *abba* or "Our Father" has stood as title for the entire Lord's Prayer and as shorthand for its content. *Abba* establishes the atmosphere of love and trust that is the hallmark of Christian prayer.

17

Hallowing: A Cry for the Kingdom

Our Father in heaven,
hallowed be your name,
your kingdom come
your will be done
*   on earth as in heaven.*

To finally know the name of God is an important leitmotif in the Old Testament. This quest surfaces as Jacob wrestles with the mysterious apparition for a blessing and for the answer to the question, "What is your name?" (Genesis 32:27). When Moses encounters the burning bush, he pleads to know God's name, saying that such knowledge will facilitate his role as mediator. So he receives from God the enigmatic name, "I Am Who I Am" (Exodus 3:14). In giving his disciples the word *abba* as a way of naming God, Jesus has revealed something of the inexpressible. Heaven's secret—to more fully know God—is revealed in the simplest word of childhood.[6]

As if to protect us from carelessness in our naming of God, the hallowing petition is closely sewn to the opening address. Indeed, Luther in *The Small Catechism* explained this petition in terms of its effect upon us:

God's name certainly is holy in itself,
but we ask in this prayer
that we may keep it holy.[7]

From Israel we learn that the best antidote for taking the name of the Lord in vain is to praise him. The *Qaddish* (Aramaic for "sanctification") ends the synagogue liturgy and would have been familiar to Jesus from his childhood. In its fervent blessing of God, this ancient prayer shows us what it means to hallow. It may well have inspired the first two petitions of the Lord's Prayer.

May his great name be magnified and sanctified
in the world that he created according to his good pleasure!
May he make his reign prevail
during your life and during your days,
and during the life of the entire house of Israel
at this very moment and very soon.
    And let them say: Amen!

May the name of the Lord—blessed be he!—
be blessed, praised, glorified, extolled,
exalted, honored, magnified, and hymned!
It is above and beyond
any blessing, hymn, praise, consolation
that men utter in this world.
    And let them say: Amen![8]

The hallowing petition involves far more than a self-conscious reminder of our need to reverence the name of God. In the hymnlike *Qaddish* as well as the Lord's Prayer we see the hallowing of God's name closely aligned with an urgent cry for God's kingdom to come and his will be done. This cry may well be the central

18

theme of the prayer and the connecting link that holds the petitions together. This beseeching of God for the eschatological deed that will finally establish his kingdom is one of the most significant motifs of the Lord's Prayer.

The Bread Petition
Give us today our daily bread

"Daily bread," wrote Luther, "includes everything needed for this life." Bread, in this petition has often been seen as an all-embracing symbol of

food and clothing, home and property,
work and income, a devoted family,
an orderly community, good government, favorable
weather, peace and health, a good name,
and true friends and neighbors.[9]

Because Jesus named himself the Bread of life and instituted a holy meal once called the "breaking of bread," it was inevitable that Christians would give some kind of eucharistic interpretation to this petition. In the year A.D. 350, a famous bishop, Cyril of Jerusalem, taught the newly baptized the meaning of the Lord's Prayer. Shorthand notes kept by one of the listeners reveal an interesting addition to the Lord's Prayer. Cyril prayed, "Give us this day our substantial bread," pointing to the bread on the altar, which "nourishes you in your entirety, for the good of body and soul."

The most tempting interpretation is the one proposed by Jeremias, Lohmeyer, and others who saw this from an eschatological perspective. There is firm evidence to support the conclusion that the Aramaic original of this petition read, "Our bread for tomorrow give us today." In other words, "Give us a taste of the great tomorrow, a foretaste of the heavenly feast."

Since primeval times, the bread of life and the water of life have been symbols of paradise, an epitome of the fulness of all God's material and spiritual gifts. It is this bread—symbol, image, and fulfillment of the age of salvation—to which Jesus is referring when he says that in the consummation he will eat and drink with his disciples (Luke 22:30) and that he will gird himself and serve them at table (Luke 12:37) with the bread which has been broken and the cup which has been blessed (cf. Matthew 26:29). The eschatological thrust of all the other petitions in the Lord's Prayer speaks for the fact that the petition for bread has an eschatological sense too (i.e., that it entreats God for the bread of life).[10]

In prayer, in poetry, and in sacred texts, words such as bread, light, or water have a multivalent quality. Our human experience of bread is compounded by a wide range of biblical meanings. There is a sense in which such prayer words ignite the imagination. One need not settle on any one interpretation but may entertain a whole breadth of meanings. "Daily bread," "substantial bread," "tomorrow's bread," all lead us more deeply into communion with the one who called himself the Bread of life.

The Forgiveness Word
Forgive us our sins
  as we forgive those
    who sin against us.

To consider this petition is to touch the heart of the gospel. To forgive in Greek *(aphiemi)* means "to remit, release, or liberate." Almost every page of the gospel accounts recount some instance of teaching or personal encounter where forgiveness is the primary theme.

As a sign of the kingdom come, Jesus reached past the social/religious taboos of his day by befriending outcasts and sinners. He not only ate with them when invited, but his enemies claimed, "This man *entertains* sinners and *feasts* with them" (Luke 15:2). This text would lead us to believe that Jesus hosted the poor and oppressed, celebrating their new respectability in his sight.

Jesus once told a middle-class host that he ought to invite "the poor, the maimed, the lame, the blind" instead of always hosting his friends and relatives (Luke 14:12-13). In the parable of the great supper (Luke 14:15-24) the invited guests made excuses, so the master of the house sent his disciples out into the streets to bring in the "poor, the maimed, the lame, and the blind." Was such teaching based on actual experience? We can assume that our Lord practiced what he preached, and the heart of that sermon was the word of forgiveness.

As he washed his disciples' feet, Jesus inaugurated the new age with the commandment to "love one another as I have loved you" (John 5:12). It is this relationship between God's deeds of love and mercy and our own willingness to imitate him that explains the petition, "Forgive us our sins *as we forgive.*" In other words, God's forgiveness is the basis for our own forgiving of others. We pass on to others the love and peace which we have received. For those who call God *abba* it is simply a necessity of our new relationship that "we on our part will heartily forgive and gladly do good to those who sin against us."[11]

The Great Anticipation

Save us from the time of trial
and deliver us from evil.

Permeating this prayer is a perspective that is almost lost on us today. Early Christians were convinced that the last days were upon them, that they soon should face the fiery trial brought on by Satan's last ditch power play against God and God's people. They also were convinced that God's kingdom would dawn upon them in great power and glory. Rather than the misconception of God as the agent of temptation, the better translation refers to that final biblical "time of trial" which marks the last days and the work of the evil one just before the final coming of God's kingdom in power and glory.

Today as always, believers stand at the center of the battle between God and the evil one. They stand on the verge of that last tomorrow, struggling with political, social, and personal powers that try to tear us away from loyalty to Christ. In moments of clarity we know we are in the same critical position as our Christian ancestors, and with them we cry out, "Save us from the time of trial, deliver us from the evil one."

Doxological Cadenza

For the kingdom, the power,
and the glory are yours,
now and forever. Amen.

In a musical composition, the cadenza was an instrumental or vocal flourish near the end of a movement of a concerto. Gradually these improvisations were written down and became an integral part of the musical text.

The same process was at work in the doxological ending of the Lord's Prayer. It is completely absent in Luke and Matthew's accounts, but it would be a mistake to think that the Lord's Prayer was ever prayed without closing words of praise to God. In Judaism it was the practice to "seal" prayers with a freely formulated doxology. Only later, as attested in the *Didache,* did that cadenza become a formal part of the text.[12]

Chapter 3

Oratio Fidelium:
The Prayer of the Faithful

Let us pray for the whole people of God in Christ Jesus and for all people according to their needs.

The *Book of Common Prayer* has exerted profound influence on the whole family of Protestant liturgies in English-speaking countries. One of the most significant revisions of the English liturgy was the 1662 *Book of Common Prayer,* which incorporated material from the newly published King James Version.

On the 300th anniversary of this liturgical text, Eric James wrote a pamphlet entitled *The Roots of Liturgy.* In a premonition of reforms that would take place in almost every major Christian community, James focused on the leitmotif of the pastoral liturgical movement:

> The greatest symbol the church possesses is perhaps that symbol which is unconsciously produced every time the church gathers: the gathered community itself, transcending race and class, color and age—the one community: the truly personal community. This is, of course, as much vision as reality, but in various ways it is evident that the church is being drawn towards the vision.[1]

The first claim of the Christian community was identity with the Jewish reality: It thought it was Israel, and for Israel the most important act of worship was the act of assembling. The root meaning of the word synagogue—"congregation, assembly"—underscores this emphasis on the gathered community.

> Religion is not what one does with solitariness; it begins in the move to overcome solitariness. Judaism lives in a social sense of reality. . . . Worship is made authentic by gathering and by the divine presence promised to devout assemblies. Indeed, God and social solidarity are so related that, even when one prays alone, the plural "we" is used in prayers; and, according to the Talmud, anyone who prays in disregard to another's prayers has his prayer "torn up before his face." The assembly of God, the synagogue, links care for God inextricably with care for neighbor.[2]

In an extensive investigation of New Testament terms that we rather indiscriminately translate as "worship," Peter Brunner comes to the conclusion that most of the familiar cultic terms—*latrei, threskei, leiturgia, duluein*—are insufficient to describe the novelty of Christian worship. The terms that most adequately express the new reality of Christian worship are those that refer to the act of assembling such as *synagesthai* (cf. Matthew 18:20—"to be assembled" in the name of Jesus) and the term *synerchesthai* (cf. 1 Corinthians 11:18, 10—"to come together" as church). In this brief word study we discern the eventful, corporate nature of early Christian prayer.[3]

This stress on the gathered community finds eloquent expression in the so-called "broken bread prayer" of the *Didache*. As part of a longer mealtime prayer that may have framed an agape meal, this gem from the earliest days of the church's life is a precious ikon of a God of harvest who graciously gathers his own "from the four winds, from one end of heaven to the other" (Matthew 24:31).

Just as the bread broken was
first scattered on the hills,
then was gathered and became one,
so let your church be gathered
from the ends of the earth into your kingdom,
for yours is glory and power through all ages.[4]

All four evangelists tell us that Jesus frequented both temple and synagogue, and we can be sure that his followers were nurtured in such an atmosphere of daily worship. In the Jerusalem community described in the Acts of the Apostles, the first followers of the way kept these patterns of temple and synagogue worship which were part of the fabric of their daily lives.

In Judaism the day was marked in the temple at Jerusalem with morning and evening sacrifice and with services of psalms and prayers at 9 A.M. and 3 P.M. Devout Jews also marked the times of the day with private prayers "in the evening, in the morning, and noonday" (Psalm 55:18). The services in the synagogue consisted principally of prayer and (at least on the Sabbath) the reading and exposition of the Scriptures. By the time of Christ the synagogue liturgy of the word was conducted on at least some weekdays as well as immediately before the Sabbath meal. Some believe that synagogues in the larger towns had daily morning and evening services.[5]

In Christian circles the various prayer "hours" were soon saturated with the remembrance of Christ's passion. A sample of this Christological theme is described in *The Apostolic Tradition of Hippolytus* from the year A.D. 215. There are times of individual or family prayer in the evening, and at midnight when "the whole creation pauses for a moment to praise the Lord." Hippolytus instructed the church of Rome to stop and pray at mid-morning "for at this hour Christ was nailed to the tree," at noon "when Christ was nailed to the wood of the cross," and at the "ninth hour" (mid-afternoon) when Christ died. The faithful were to greet the dawn with prayer as an everlasting remembrance of the resurrection.[6]

A most important element of this account was the opportunity to gather the entire community for daily prayer and instruction on the word of God. Hippolytus makes it clear that this was a mandatory experience for the well-being of individual and community.

At agape mealtime, Sunday Eucharist, and in periods of daily prayer, the corporate nature of prayer was underscored and stressed. Those who formed the biblical accounts and shaped the life of the early church believed that prayer in community was prayer par excellence. Here was the "place" where life with God and with others was augmented, intensified—"where the Spirit is strongly present."[7] To underscore the recovery of this aspect of Christian worship is a priority in our day.

23

Some would claim that "Christian prayer is always and only corporate prayer; it is prayer of the community or it is not prayer at all."[8]

Common prayer is essentially Christian because it challenges preoccupation with self and heightens our awareness of others. In community, love of neighbor is invited and nourished. From common prayer grows one of the purest forms of Christian expression—prayer for others, intercessory prayer. While this element is present in varied circumstances of Christian worship, nowhere does it find more intentional expression than in that part of the Sunday eucharistic liturgy historically labeled the *oratio fidelium,* the prayer of the faithful.

Since this public intercession is a paradigm for intercessory expression in Christian life, we need to know something of its origin, its deformation and loss, and the present day insistence on its recovery. The remainder of this chapter is devoted to a capsule summary of the liturgical history of what has variously been referred to by names such as the Prayer of the Faithful, the Prayer of the Church, the Prayers of the People, or General Intercessions.

Those who study the origins of intercessory prayer in the life of the church point to the seminal influence of the ancient *Shemone Esre Berakot* or "Eighteen Blessings." Simply called *Tefillah* or the "Prayer," it was "the most official and most representative prayer of Judaism."[9] This great prayer was prayed in morning, afternoon, and evening services of the synagogue and recited three times a day by pious Jews. Another title, *Amidah* or "standing" describes the congregational posture of standing with arms raised and actively voicing their involvement with acclamations and amens.

Punctuated by formulas of blessing, the overarching emphasis of this prayer is on praise and thanksgiving. Penitential elements, such as "Forgive us, O our Father, for we have sinned against you," conclude with the beatitude, "Blessed are you, Lord, you hasten to multiply forgiveness." Petitions for individual need end with the assurance, "Blessed are you, Lord, you hear our prayers." Intercessions for the peace of Israel, the people, the city of Jerusalem are balanced with the promise and conviction, "Then together we shall praise you. Blessed are you, Lord, you give us peace." The continual refrain of blessing makes each petition a reason to praise and a sign of the expected grace of God.

St. Paul's letters give abundant evidence to this praise–prayer connection in the early church. Almost every epistle begins with a statement such as:

I thank my God in all my remembrance of you, always in every prayer of mine for you all making my prayer with joy, thankful for your partnership in the gospel from the first day until now (Philippians 1:3-5).

Typical of the literary convention of his day, Paul thanked his God for some blessing related to the letter's subject, and then he went on to pray for the reader's good health and well-being.

And it is my prayer that your love may abound more and more, with knowledge and all discernment, so that you may approve what is excellent, and may be pure and blameless for the day of Christ (Philippians 1:9-10).

It has been suggested that Paul not only includes these statements as token moments of praise and prayer, but he also lets them serve as the dominating theme of

24

the teaching and exhortation that follows in the body of the letter. In other words, the letter becomes an explication of the thanksgiving prayer preamble.

Paul and other leaders not only pray for the strengthening of those early congregations, but they also call for partnership in this ministry of intercession.

First of all, then, I urge that supplications, prayers, intercessions, and thanksgivings be made for all men, for kings and all who are in high positions, that we may lead a quiet and peaceable life, godly and respectful in every way. This is good, and it is acceptable in the sight of God our Savior, who desires all men to be saved and to come to the knowledge of the truth. For there is one God, and there is one mediator between God and men, the man Christ Jesus, who gave himself as a ransom for all, the testimony to which was borne at the proper time (1 Timothy 2:1-7).

In Justin Martyr's famous account of Christian worship around Rome in the year A.D. 150, we are shown a community gathering on the Sun's Day to hear the memoirs of the apostles, the writings of the prophets, and a presider's address based on those readings. Between this germinal liturgy of the Word and the offering of bread, wine, and water for the Eucharist, Justin states, "We all stand and pray." In another section of his *Apologia* for Christian life and worship, he describes the process of Christian initiation. After the baptismal washing, those who have been "enlightened" and "cleansed" are taken from the place of water to the Christian assembly where, he writes:

We offer prayers in common for ourselves, for him who has just been enlightened, and for all men everywhere. It is our desire, now that we have come to know the truth, to be found worthy of doing good deeds and obeying the commandments, and thus to obtain eternal salvation. When we finish praying, we greet one another with a kiss.[11]

The earliest actual wording of such intercessory prayer in Christian worship comes from St. Clement's *Letter to the Corinthians*. Written about A.D. 95-98, this letter from the Bishop of Rome concludes with what has come to be called the Great Prayer. Like the *Shemone Esre* it is saturated with ascriptions of praise which contain distinctive moments of intercession:

Save the afflicted among us,
have mercy on the lowly.
Raise up the fallen,
show yourself to those in need.
Heal the sick
and bring back those who have strayed.
Fill the hungry,
give freedom to our prisoners,
raise up the weak,
console the fainthearted.[12]

By the third century the intercessions were a recognizable "set piece" following readings and sermon and concluding the synaxis (the service of gathering and the Word). In his study of "Intercession at the Eucharist," Jardine Grisbrook says that "historically there can be no doubt that this was its universal ancient position, and psychologically intercession should follow instruction rather than precede it."[13]

In those early days of rigorous catechumenate, members-in-process were not allowed to pray in common with the congregation or to participate in the Eucharist. Their dismissal in the liturgy came just before the general intercessions and peace. The so-called Mass of the Faithful actually began with the Prayer of the Faithful (*oratio fidelium*) which technically concluded the synaxis. This prayer, therefore, can be seen as a hinge between the two major aspects of Sunday worship: it concludes the liturgy of the Word in which God's wonderful acts are celebrated, and it ushers in the liturgy of the eucharistic meal as its intentions are ritually described in community meal and breaking of bread.[14]

Scholars believe that a form of this early prayer of the faithful has survived from the third century to the present day in the solemn prayers that conclude the liturgy of Good Friday. Nine times the president of the assembly invites the congregation to pray. After each bid, a deacon directs the people to kneel and to devote themselves to silent prayer. Then, again at the deacon's direction, all rise as the priest leads a short "collecting prayer" (*collecta*). The congregation, together with the leader, expresses their assent with a loud "Amen."

> It is probably correct to say that this form of prayer successfully combined the silent devotion of the individual and the vocal prayer of the congregation and in addition also helped the people to give themselves both in body and soul to the service of God.[15]

In the Roman rite, the ancient intercession was made up of nine biddings and prayers.

1. for the church
2. for the pope or presiding bishop
3. for all ministers of the church
4. for the Roman emperor
5. for the catechumens
6. for those in any trouble
7. for heretics and schismatics
8. for the Jews
9. for the heathen[16]

In other areas, intercessions were expanded to include a wide range of concerns such as the rising of the Nile, readers and singers, temperate weather and good harvests, and "little ones of the church." In the Syrian rite in the "Apostolic Constitutions" there are no less than 21 diaconal biddings.[17]

Near the end of the fifth century, Pope Gelasius I borrowed from the Eastern churches another form of intercessory prayer. A deacon would announce the subject of intercession and the congregation responded, *"Kyrie eleison"* ("Lord, have mercy"). This form proved to be attractive because it was easily understood and possessed a lively rhythm. Gelasius introduced it in the mass as a replacement for the older form of intercessory prayer and moved it from the Liturgy of the Faithful to the beginning of the Liturgy of the Catechumens. By this time, however, the catechumenate and its disciplines had come to an end, so that it seemed unnecessary to bar the unbaptized from participation in common prayer.

Over a century later, Pope Gregory the Great worked to abbreviate the mass, which then could last for as long as three hours. In his efficiency campaign, he shortened the intercessory litany inherited from Gelasius and on certain nonfestival days completely dispensed with the deacon's bid, retaining only the remnant response, "Kyrie eleison. Christe eleison."

As the ancient prayer of the faithful withered to a few token words, there was a parallel tendency to pick up intercessory elements in the canon or eucharistic prayer. Such intercession took the form of diptychs (a list of the names of those who brought offerings and a list of the names of the departed who were remembered and who might benefit by these gifts). The idea developed that such intentions and intercessions were more effective if they were imbedded in the eucharistic prayer. The influential Cyril of Jerusalem, for instance, taught that "we believe that these souls will obtain greatest help if we make our prayers for them while the holy and most awesome sacrifice is being offered."[18]

To enshrine the major intercessory element of the liturgy in the eucharistic prayer severely diminished the corporate expression of this prayer. As clerical domain, it did not allow for participation by the people. Gradually the canon of the mass became more and more fixed and general in nature. Eventually, as a sign of reverence, it was whispered by the celebrant, thus silencing intercession in the mass from the sixth century until the restoration of the prayer of the faithful in our own day.

There are always exceptions to such generalizations. Some French churches continued a prayer of the people after the Gospel. In Germany and Bohemia evidence survives of a preaching service named Prone with an intercessory element termed the Bidding of the Bedes. In this vernacular prayer, the priest announced the subject. The people prayed the "Our Father" silently as the priest went on to solemnly pray a collect before introducing the next subject. This bidding prayer may have been the sole surviving intercessory component in the liturgy, prompting the 16th century reformers to reinstate some form of universal intercessory prayer in their liturgies.

In his first major liturgical revision, the *Formula Missae,* Luther made no reference to a general prayer of intercession. In the *Deutsch Messe* of 1526, he introduced a paraphrase of the Lord's Prayer, which followed the sermon. Luther also revised the Litany of All Saints and promoted this sung prayer at matins and vespers or after a sermon. With these proposals and their previous exposure to Prone, Lutheran church orders gradually developed a form of general church prayer or *Allgemeine Kirchengebet* which consisted of comprehensive intercessory petitions.

In developing and incorporating such a general intercession in the liturgy proper, the Reformation actually—though perhaps not consciously—restored the essential features of the ancient "Prayer of the Faithful."

By broadening petitions it gave new emphasis and importance to the idea of a general prayer as such. By introducing new thanksgivings and petitions concerning the Word and its fruitfulness, it stressed Lutheran ideas. By inserting brief responses at the end of sections it gave the whole prayer a distinct congregational character.[19]

In England, Archbishop Cranmer consolidated scattered intercessory material into one prayer, "For the Whole State of Christ's Church." Though Cranmer first placed this prayer after the *Sanctus* (Holy, holy, holy Lord God), he later transferred it away from its close proximity to the Eucharist and put it after the offertory to conclude the antecommunion. Like Luther, this great English liturgiologist reshaped a fine litany and encouraged its use as a conclusion to Morning Prayer or as prelude to the Eucharist. This litany had great strengths and weaknesses. Although it was evangelically sound and comprehensive, its great length, rigidity, and penitential flavor worked against its popularity.

Intercessory prayer in the "free church" stream of Protestant experience can only be accurately portrayed by tracing the history of each denomination or faith community. While such a task is far beyond the scope of this work, it is still reasonable to list some characteristics of this movement found in Zwingli, the Anabaptists, and later embraced by German pietists, English and American Puritans, Baptists, Quakers, and many other related communities. In our own day, the free church approach to public prayer has influenced not only evangelical and charismatic Christians, but it also has been adopted in a few so-called liturgical churches.

Insisting that prayer should come "from the heart," the free churches have usually rejected written and set forms of prayers in public as well as individual circumstances. This stance suspects liturgy of trying to compete with Scripture and of robbing the worshiper of personal understanding and honest experience in prayer. Some of the more radical Puritans repudiated all preconceived prayers and even refused to use the Lord's Prayer. In other camps some premeditation in public prayer is accepted as a more disciplined way of ordering the prayers of the church.

From 17th century New England come accounts of Puritan worship that expresses such concerns. A contemporary observer described worship that began with a lengthy pastoral prayer ("about a quarter of an hour"). The congregation stood with uplifted hands for this and all prayers that were extemporaneously spoken. Puritan John Cotton described this long opening period of prayer by the pastor:

> First then when we come together in the church, according to the apostle direction, 1 Timothy 2:1, we make prayers and intercessions and thanksgivings for ourselves and for all men, not in any prescribed form of prayer or studied liturgy, but in such a manner as the Spirit of grace and of prayer (who teacheth all the people of God, what and how to pray, Romans 8:26-27) helpeth our infirmities, we having respect therein to the necessities of the people; the estate of the times, and the work of Christ in our hands.[20]

In our own day, contemporary liturgical revision has displayed a strong trend toward restoring some form of the prayer of the faithful to its place as offertory hinge between synaxis (service of gathering and the Word) and the liturgy of the eucharistic meal. Years of research and shared insights have moved the ecumenical community to a new concern for intercessory prayer in public worship as well as in the spirituality of Christian people. The next two chapters of this book will propose ways and means of energizing a ministry of intercession.

Chapter 4

Intercession:
Praying the World to God

First of all, then, I urge that supplications, prayers, intercessions, and thanks-givings be made for all men, for kings and all who are in high positions, that we may lead a quiet and peaceable life, godly and respectful in every way (1 Timothy 2:1-2).

I appeal to you, brethren, by our Lord Jesus Christ and by the love of the Spirit, to strive together with me in your prayers to God (Romans 15:30).

New Testament references to intercessory prayer surprise us with their passionate language. "I appeal to you . . . strive with me." Paul's charge to the congregation in Rome has the force of an earnest questing together in prayer.

A century later, Tertullian (A.D. 160-220) used a military image to express the urgent nature of this aspect of corporate worship.

We come together for a meeting and a congregation in order to besiege God with prayers, like an army in battle formation. We pray also for the emperors, for their ministers and those in power.[1]

Luther, who spoke of prayer as a "great almighty thing," encouraged the congregations of his day to pray fervently and expectantly:

We must take to heart the needs of all people and pray for them in real sympathy and in true faith and trust. Oh, if any congregation were to pray in this way, so that a common, earnest, heartfelt cry of the whole people were to rise up to God, what immeasurable virtue and help would result from such a prayer![2]

In the public assembly as in individual prayer, we often neglect the dynamic of intercession. There is little real asking and certainly no storming of heaven with our petitions. For many worshipers the prayer of the faithful is just one more piece of liturgical line that stretches from greeting to dismissal with little conscious variation. We rarely reach through these forms to sense the spiritual voltage beneath the surface. We need to rethink this matter of "praying the world to God" and find patterns that will make for renewal in this important Christian ministry.

"Intercession," said Martin Marty, "is loving your neighbor on your knees." In other words, intercessory prayer and our social ministry are made of the same cloth. In intercession the essential connection between liturgy and life is made and celebrated. Nowhere else do we give such regular ritual focus to this intersection and to the missionary impulse at the heart of Christian worship.

Corporate intercessory prayer rescues us from the ambit of purely personal concern and draws us into the crucible of Christian ministry. Each time we pray for others we undergo a mini-conversion, a liberation from self. We are turned away from self to look in the direction that God is looking.[3] To pray the world to God—

remembering the needs of hungry, poor, the dying, nations at war, societies in disarray, nature contaminated by waste—is to sense something of our solidarity with God's creation and with those for whom Christ died. That identification wakens the remembrance of the responsibility given us in the beginning when we were called to be caretakers of creation.

Early Christians prayed fervently for the church and its ministry to the world. To remember before God the faith community is to pledge ourselves to the vision of unity and peace for which we pray. Our prayers flow through and around institutional and theoretical barriers to effect an experience of Christian love.

> Intercession is an expression of fellowship in Christ and, at the same time, a means of strengthening it. In intercession we bring our fellow Christians before God and ask that his name be glorified in them.[4]

We pray because God has promised to hear and to answer our prayers. Beyond the natural benefits we derive from the mere act of prayer, the elementary matter of prayer as asking and receiving needs to be affirmed. How easily we succumb to psychological treatments of prayer that avoid the New Testament's childlike expectation, "Ask, and it will be given you." Without this simple understanding, prayer has no wings; it is grounded on the floor of our sophisticated explanations.

In the worship assembly, our prayers envision a world at peace, creation healed and cherished, and a community of faith living out the life of Christ. With such prayer we picture a society beyond our fondest dreams. In effect we embrace a biblical picture of God's "kingdom come." Intercession is an eschatological act. We groan with the whole cosmos for the final liberation from sin and death. And those who intercede stand as living reminders of the hope and goal of our faith.

One of the most significant developments in the recovery of intercession in Christian life and worship has been the restoration of the ancient prayer of the faithful in the Sunday assembly. While we voice this theme in daily prayer and in other nonsacramental services, its primary location is in this "universal prayer" that concludes the service of the word and simultaneously participates in the first act of the eucharistic meal. The prayers not only hinge the two parts of the service of Holy Communion, but they also hinge our experience of corporate and individual prayer. Public worship has always served as a "school for prayer," the time when the church models such disciplines as intercession and teaches its people how to pray.

The *Constitution on the Sacred Liturgy* from Vatican II brought into focus years of liturgical research. The document articulated not only a liturgical direction for the Roman Catholics, but it also affected other mainline Christian communities that share a common liturgical tradition.

> Especially on Sundays and holy days of obligation there is to be restored, after the Gospel and the homily, "the universal prayer" or "the prayer of the faithful." By this prayer, in which the people are to take part, intercession shall be made for holy church, for the civil authorities, for those oppressed by various needs, for all people, and for the salvation of the entire world.[5]

In a survey of denominational worship texts such as the American *Book of Common Prayer* and *Lutheran Book of Worship,* and in recent international worship

30

events, one finds a broad ecumenical consensus concerning the content and conduct of prayers of intercession. The following list attempts to characterize the major elements of this new consensus on the reintroduction of the prayer of the faithful. These capsule statements will serve as outline for the commentary that concludes this chapter.

In the liturgical usage of differing traditions the Prayer of the Faithful has been variously called the Prayer of the Church, the Prayer of the People, the General Intercessions, the Universal Prayer, the Intercessions, and just The Prayers.

These prayers may be introduced either by an assisting or presiding minister who asks an introductory bid and gives a concluding collect. The primary agent of intercession, however, should be a deacon, cantor, or non-ordained assisting minister.

So that the prayer of the faithful may be an authentic expression of a given community—universal and yet at home in every time and place—there is a strong preference for freedom in its formulation.

The prayers should be prepared for each service by those in the local community who have recognized gifts and who are charged with the responsibility for this ministry.

A principal element of the prayer of the faithful is the participation of the people by way of short acclamations, responses, silent prayer, or communal recitation.

Language, format, and style of leadership are vital areas of concern for the effectiveness of the intercessions in public liturgy.

Traditionally the intentions of this prayer include petitions for the members and ministry of the universal church, the nation and all in authority, the salvation of the world, those who suffer and are oppressed, the concerns of the local community, and the departed.

The Role of Intercessor

The assembling of a congregation for worship is . . . an assembling of Christian ministers who bring the concerns of their ministries with them. In the intercessions these concerns are gathered and placed before God, thus uniting prayer and service. Corporate worship should involve different persons in such ministries of liturgical leadership as reading lessons, leading prayers, assisting in the distribution of bread and wine, receiving the offering, choral singing, and planning the services. The variety of liturgical ministries expresses the variety of gifts in a community, and symbolizes the participational character of the gathered church.[6]

In the beginning, the church was marked by a diversity of gifts as people exercised varied ministries. There was simply no word to distinguish, as we do today, between clergy and laity. All were party of the *"laos," "a chosen race, a royal priesthood, a holy nation."* As Hans Küng observed, the New Testament clearly avoids using terms which denote primacy or rank in reference to Christian ministry.[7] The contemporary affirmation of ministries and their liturgical expression is a sign that we are recovering the "participational character of the gathered church" and that "liturgy is the celebration of all who gather together."

When Martin Luther wrote "To the Christian Nobility," he powerfully underscored the priestly character of all the baptized, saying, "whoever comes out of the water of Baptism can boast that he is already a consecrated priest, bishop, and pope."[8] This general priesthood, he wrote, "makes us worthy to stand before God and pray for others."[9]

Intercessory prayer is one of the basic baptismal rights and responsibilities of the Christian life. In the early church, a sign of the connection between Baptism and intercessory prayer came in one of the first gifts of Baptism. Formerly excluded from the prayer of the faithful, the newly baptized were able to participate in this prayer which also served as entree to the fellowship of the Eucharist. The close proximity of the prayers, the peace, and the offering is a natural and provocative one. In some literature, the prayers have been contextualized as an offertory element because they spring from the same basic motivation—to remember the world to God.

As in the offering of the gifts of bread and wine, so the intercessions grow out of everyday life—wherever the people of God find themselves during the week.

It is no accident that this particular moment . . . should be the special charge of the laity, for it is a movement that must have its origin at the very heart of the everyday world of work and leisure. The offertory . . . should not start in the sanctuary—if it does our religion is losing its roots in the stuff and muck of life.

What we are doing at the offertory is simply letting God get his hand on . . . that . . . which is represented by our lives, so that through us, his new community, the whole world with which it is in contact may ultimately be changed.[10]

In leading the prayer of the faithful, the intercessor embodies these profound themes. As a diaconal or lay leader, the intercessor communicates a sense of solidarity with those who join in common prayer. This solidarity extends beyond the worship assembly to common patterns of life at the office or factory, in home or school.

This is a highly sensitive role, for the way a person leads prayer is a reflection of what he or she believes. To engage in liturgical speaking and acting is to take a position on a wide range of theological topics. And if this person is to be believed, the words of prayer will have to be accompanied by a demonstration of active ministry. As Geoffrey Wainwright says: "The test of sincere intercession is the commitment to corresponding action."[11]

The intercessor must be carefully selected by the pastoral and congregational leadership on the basis of recognized gifts, communication skills, spiritual depth, and involvement in the life and ministry of the congregation. While this person may fulfill a general diaconal or lay assisting minister role in the liturgy, it is preferable to concentrate on their responsibility as prayer leader.

A standing program of study, prayer, and practical experience will be necessary for those who would take this role seriously. The chapters of this book along with other selected works on prayer could serve as texts for a four- or five-week course tailored to a local situation. There should be discussion of the content, form, and language of liturgical prayer as well as extended practice.

At the heart of this program would be the opportunity to pray and to nurture the discipline of individual prayer. Talking about prayer is not enough; one must become confident and comfortable in praying with others. A minimal requirement for those who accept this call would be to have a recognizable pattern of daily prayer already established. Without the spiritual sustenance that comes from family, group, or individual prayer, it is dangerous to pretend the role of congregational intercessor.

Initially a team of four or five people could be trained and commissioned for this ministry. It is important to style this as a "term commitment," lest intercession be seen as the prerogative of the gifted few rather than the property of the people. Initially a team of four or five men and women could rotate their leadership over a period of six months before integrating a second group into the process.

Fixed Form Versus Free Prayer

Any discussion of the content, form, and language of intercessory prayer in public worship must deal with the question of fixed form versus extempore prayer. Rubrical advice in the liturgical texts of two major American denominations reveal divergent approaches to the subject. Referring to the Prayer of the Church, *Lutheran Book of Worship* instructs: "Preparation of the prayers is no less important than preparation of the sermon."[12]

This directive is not only a strong indicator of the renewed importance of public intercessory prayer but reveals an expectation regarding prayer formation and presentation. In Lutheran circles sermons do not just happen; there is considerable premeditation and preparation. For several centuries the sermon has been the preeminent component of Lutheran liturgies. So the statement above is a little astounding and quite challenging to those who take the time to read such advice.

It should be admitted that few Lutheran congregations exert the kind of energy required by that liturgical note. In most instances, the Prayer of the Church is borrowed intact from bulletin inserts, worshipbooks, or collections of altar prayers. The names of the sick may be inserted in the petition for the sick, but that is often the extent of any variation or indigenous shaping of these models. The use of extempore prayer or the creative adaptation of prefabricated forms are lost in the rush to fill that slot in the liturgy.

On the other hand, a supplemental resource of the United Methodist Church simply invites: Concerns may be spoken spontaneously, to which all make common response, such as "Lord, hear our prayer." *Or,* a pastoral prayer may be offered."[13]

Here, the preference in both options is weighted in the direction of free prayer, prayer offered "according to one's ability."

In the Jewish milieu that shaped early Christian directions in worship, rabbis spoke of these two contrasting themes in prayer in terms of *kavvanah* and *keva*.

Kavvanah is spontaneous prayer—inward, pure, devout, concentrated, and free.

Kavvanah is the necessary ingredient of true prayer. *Keva,* on the other hand, is traditional prayer. It is the prayer of routine. It gives continuity to the liturgical tradition. It is what makes prayer recognizable as Jewish prayer. We all recognize this dynamic from experience: we find our identity as a Roman Catholic or an Episcopalian or a Lutheran in a certain continuity of form in the tradition.

The rabbinic commentaries on *kavvanah,* spontaniety, and *keva,* tradition, always held out as an ideal that traditional prayer should be invested with the spirit of spontaneous prayer.[14]

According to evidence from this germinal period, the primitive Christian liturgy flourished in the harmonious relationship of both spontaneous prayer and fixed, traditional forms. In his study on the history of freedom and formula in worship, Alan Bouley calls this a time of "guided freedom" in which customary forms were handled with flexibility and spontaneity. Even when Hippolytus gives his famous prototype of eucharistic prayer, he hastens to add:

Let the bishop give thanks in the manner we indicated earlier. It is not necessary, however, that he repeat the same words we provided, as though he had to try to say them from memory in his thanksgiving to God. Let each one pray according to his ability. If he is capable of praying at length and offering a solemn prayer, well and good. But if he prays differently and pronounces a shorter and simpler prayer, he is not to be prevented, provided his prayer be sound and orthodox.[15]

In an established faith community, church history reveals the gradual victory of *keva* or *kavvanah,* of uniformity over variety, of the fixed form over the spontaneous expression.

If for some reason that community experiences some form of insurrection, the resulting faction will often embrace methods that epitomize their newfound freedom. A more charismatic approach to prayer and worship often typifies such movements. But when one looks at all of this from the long perspective, it is clear that both fixed form and free prayer are important elements. Many would argue that good liturgy is "a fusion, a joining, a marriage of these two elements."[16] Certainly an item on the agenda of the liturgical movement today is the need to examine and test the growing rapprochement between the sometimes disparate tendencies of fixed form and free prayer.

Preparation to Presentation

Careful preparation of the prayers and Spirit-led presentation are not mutually exclusive forces, but they are the necessary ingredients in fulfilling the expectations of intercessory prayer in public worship. This approach combines the strengths of both traditional, fixed form and free prayer, attempting to rediscover the early ideal of "guided freedom" in the prayers. Exploring the potential and problems of this ideal can lead to a more informed prayer practice.

When intercessors base their work on printed, prefabricated prayers, they have the advantage of using forms that have well-considered language, scriptural soundness, and catholic breadth. These forms of prayer allow for more faithful expression than if one were simply mentioning the unshaped impressions of the moment. When such prayers are printed for the congregation they invite the people into deeper participation and appreciation of their own role. As noble as such prayers may be, however, they must be owned by the local community or they will be liturgically impotent. Fixed forms of intercessory prayer should prompt and guide, but never dominate us.

One of the contributions of the free-prayer tradition is the reminder that prayer is primarily an act rather than a composition to be read. Public prayer is an oral medium; it lives in the vocative mode.

It is like music which exists to be performed and heard. The written musical notes are a prompter of sounds to be played or sung, and, in the case of ensemble works, they are a device to let many people take part together. But the music on the page is only latent until it is performed. Music is an act in time. The free-prayer tradition has maintained a similar sense of prayer as something done—and done in that biblical totality of "heart" and "lips."[17]

Intuitive, charismatic prayer is often engaging because it moves from generalities to the concrete and specific. It takes on the flesh and blood of genuine human intentions.

Written prayer is so often read rather than prayed. Charismatic prayer, on the other hand, is convincing because it feels like praying rather than the reading of a text. Prayer, finally, is in the praying and not just in the composition. This spiritual energy comes not only from a style of leadership but also from the ability of free prayer to easily reach out and grasp the exigencies of a particular situation.

As invigorating as extempore prayer may be in some communities, it is more embarrassing than edifying in others. Our model in this matter, the free flowing "pastoral prayer" is often characterized by hackneyed expressions, shallow theology, and idiosyncratic ramblings that put the congregation at the mercy of the leader's moods. It is often an insult to the assembly and an evasion of responsibility to simply "leave it to the Spirit" in such moments of public prayer.

When entire communities are invited into free-form prayer, there are many reasons for the failure of what would seem to be an ideal—the prayer of the people by the people! A large barn of a building will swallow up the voices of people who have not been trained to project their voices in public gatherings. Passing a microphone involves technical problems, and moving people to a microphone is often a distraction. Sometimes the content of such prayer is inappropriate. Is it pastorally responsible for someone to reveal to the congregation the nature of another's illness? Is it God's will to "bless America" to the exclusion of all the other nations in God's care? Should the Christian community tacitly listen and pray for victory for the high school football team?

At the heart of this problem is the tendency for group prayer to become a public praying of private prayer. The assembly stumbles over the use of first person singular pronouns, the idiosyncrasies of individual petitions, and the inability to successfully cue the congregational responses. More serious is the inclination of some people to grasp the moment as a soapbox for their special causes which may, in fact, have little support in the assembly. People complain that they do not know how to pray, and that certainly extends to the public realm. Only a concerted program of teaching and modeling prayer will enable our people to confidently offer their prayers in such a highly charged situation as the public liturgy of the church. Without such training, it is irresponsible to force them into the kind of participation for which they are not prepared.

Between the poles of printed and extemporaneous prayer, congregations have devised different ways of gathering and presenting the prayers. A box, a sign-up sheet, or book in the narthex may serve as a collector of local petitions. In one congregation, a special book of intercession is ritually presented to the prayer leader who then incorporates its contents into the prayers. In another situation, pew racks contain three-by-five-inch cards which may be filled out and placed in the offering plate; then the intercessor incorporates those petitions into the prayers. These ideas not only strain the logistics of a situation, but they also challenge the ingenuity of the one who must spontaneously integrate such concerns into the prayer.

A more desirable approach to gathering the prayers is this: The intercessor of the week would establish a network of people who become sources, supplying the concerns that should be included in the prayer of the faithful. Pastor, congregational leaders, other intercessors, and friends can help the prayer leader balance the "universal scope proper to Christian concern with the specific concerns of a given congregation." Such collaboration, which could take place in a standing weekly meeting or over the telephone, would insure a corporate shaping of both content and language of the prayers. While each congregation must finally find its own way of gathering the intentions and petitions of the people, some form of intentional program is a necessity if it is to be the prayer of the faithful.

Liturgical leadership is a complex act that involves far more than the transmission of verbal data. Body language, facial expression, tone of voice, and the influence of the environment often have more impact than the cognitive content of the message. It is, therefore, not enough for the prayer leader to come to the assembly only with the right words, but an appreciation of the many languages that will help or hinder the performance of this role is also necessary. Peripheral but influencial matters that need to be considered and finally decided by the demands and expectations of the local situation are:

> To be vested as other liturgical ministers are expresses the baptismal equality of all who lead worship. Vestments cover our peculiarities and are often signs of the varied responsibilities in liturgy. On the other hand, wearing "everyday clothes" speaks of the radical identification of the intercessor with the people and his or her representative function.

> The intercessor may accompany the other worship leaders throughout the liturgy or may come forth from the congregation at the time of the prayer. When there is no communion, the intercessor might come forward with the gifts, bearing the book of intercessions.

> The prayers may be led from the midst of the congregation, from the chairs of the leadership party, or near the altar. If a font is visible and in close proximity to the chancel area, the prayers might be led from this physical sign of Christian ministry.

Several people may lead the prayers, or prayer petitions may be spoken by a variety of voices from the congregation.

If the prayer leader uses notes or written pages, the material should be held in a special folder or book of intercessions rather than held as loose leaf material. In no case should prayers be read as one would read a lesson from desk or lectern. Any obvious dependency on written material may detract from the nature of this prayer.

Normally the leader and congregation stand for the prayers, with the option of kneeling during certain penitential seasons. The intercessor should not kneel alone or adopt a different posture from that of the assembly. Freedom in such matters of physical expression usually depends on the size and nature of the group. A small, family-sized group may feel at home praying together with open hands or by holding hands, but a large gathering may need formality and restraint.

The intercessory theme is found in various areas of worship (i.e. the Kyrie in gathering rite, intercession in Great Thanksgiving. Intercession finds its primary expression in the prayer of the faithful. Therefore, if it is desirable to eliminate one part of worship which includes intercession, the Kyrie could be eliminated; the prayer of the faithful should be kept.

A tandem relationship of confessional and intercessory prayer may be occasioned by sermon, season, or pastoral discernment, but it is usually undesirable as a regular component of the prayer of the faithful.

There are opportunities for intercession in the daily prayer offices and occasional services (e.g., marriage). While most of the recommendations of this chapter have focused on the leadership of the prayer of the faithful, they generally hold true for any instance of public intercessory prayer.

The prayer leader orchestrates the prayers rather than simply saying or even praying petitions. A deliberate pace is essential if the congregation is to accompany the intercessor in prayer. Spaces must be left for reflection, silent prayer, and when appropriate, free prayer. Voice, body, and personality all participate in the spirit and impact of this prayer. Intercessors should seek out the response of others to their leadership style so that they can become more effective in this ministry.

Chapter 5

Guidelines:
The Practice of Public Prayer

Lord Jesus Christ, Son of God,
*   we implore you to hear us.*
Lamb of God, you take away the sin of the world;
*   have mercy on us.*
Lamb of God, you take away the sin of the world;
*   give us peace. Amen.*

In this book, texts of several intercessory prayers are presented. Using those texts as examples, this chapter is a running commentary on the subjects of content, form, and language proper to the Prayer of the Faithful. It is hoped that this approach will help intercessors adapt and form prayers that are indigenous to the local congregation, and not just copy prefabricated prayers.

Introductory Address

Normally the presiding minister introduces the prayers with a formula such as: "Let us pray for the whole people of God in Christ Jesus, and for all people according to their needs."[1]

Whether this common formula is used or one freely devised, the people should feel genuinely invited into prayer. This introduction may touch on the themes of church year or feast day, or it may propose congregational responses. In any case it should be brief. On occasion it may be omitted.

The Intentions

To encourage variety and specificity, *Lutheran Book of Worship* does not specify one fixed formulation for the prayers but notes that "they must be prepared for each service." The rubrical notes indicate that:

Prayers are included for the whole church, the nations, those in need, the parish, special concerns.

The congregation may be invited to offer petitions and thanksgivings.

Prayers of confession may be included in the Brief Order for Confession and Forgiveness that have not been used earlier.

The minister gives thanks for the faithful departed, especially for those who recently have died.[2]

In the section entitled "Petitions, Intercessions, and Thanksgivings," *Lutheran Book of Worship* records an example of the Prayer of the Church (Form A).[3] Formal and fulsome, it is a rendition of the Lutheran general prayer or predecessor *All-gemeine Kirchengebet.*

In the best Judeo-Christian tradition, this prayer begins and ends in a doxological key. The blessing motif is strongly represented by such phrases as "with gladness we give thanks for all your goodness. We bless you. . . . We praise you. . . . We thank you. . . . Help us to treasure in our hearts all that our Lord has done for us, and enable us to show our thankfulness by lives that are wholly given to your service." As such it reminds us that the prayer of the faithful ought to include elements of thanksgiving, supplications for ourselves, as well as intercession for others. It is recorded here, however, as a worthy example of a prayer that remembers in its contents the classic categories of public intercessory prayer.

Based on historical study and a broad ecumenical survey, these general categories might be set forth as follows:

> The need of the church universal (for bishops and pastors of the Church, other areas of leadership and Christian vocation, missions, Christian unity, church schools).

> The welfare of nation and world (peace, justice, enemies, leaders of government and international organizations, elections, the safety of crops, famine, economic crises, good weather, care of the earth).

> Those beset by special needs (for the poor, the persecuted, the unemployed, the sick and infirm, the lonely, the dying, prisoners, exiles).

> The concerns of the local community (those preparing for baptism, confirmation, marriage, going on retreat, for a coming parish program).

> The faithful departed (congregational members, relatives, community friends who have recently died, commemoration of a saint when appropriate).[4]

Only under exceptional circumstances would one lead this prayer as printed. Despite the inclusion of congregational response, its length and stately language may disable congregational participation. So much depends on the nature of the people, their needs, the style of the liturgy and its leadership. Listening to the language of this prayer, adopting certain themes and adapting others is a prudent way to use such models. A primary contribution of this prayer is its ability to address the general categories of intercessory prayer without exhausting that area of concern. Each Sunday gives us fresh opportunities to expand upon a given motif and to focus on a specific aspect of that theme.

The Format

It is generally believed that an early form of the prayer of the faithful is remembered in the solemn Bidding Prayer of the Good Friday liturgy. In ancient usage as in the contemporary revision (Form B), a deacon or assisting minister announces the subject for prayer. After the people pray in silence, the presiding minister gathers the prayer together in a short collect. A new subject is given, and the process is repeated. It is traditional for the congregation to stand for the biddings and to kneel during the silence and the prayers. Physically and spiritually the people are drawn into this shared prayer on Good Friday where it is a centerpiece of the worship service.

This format—invitation, silence, collecting prayer—is still a highly recommended form for intercessory prayer. Following this approach, responsorial prayers (Form C) have been published for each Sunday of the three-year cycle. Richard Mazziota, who has published a modern collection of prayers, argues that, along with a commitment to this form, these general intercessions need "to emerge as unambiguously from the readings as the homily should." While this thematic approach seasonally colors the intentions and makes for variety, it should hardly be considered a ground rule for the formulations of public intercessory prayer.

Congregational Assent

A hallmark of the prayers printed in the Appendix is their statements of intention. These statements invite the people into the spirit and meaning of the prayer. The internal assent of all who enter common prayer is an absolute necessity if this act is to be more than the solitary prayer of the intercessor.

These statements of intention may be voiced by presiding or assisting ministers as a listing of the prayer requests or as prefatory invitations that introduce the categories of prayer, following the ancient model just discussed. Another option is the responsorial prayer, in which the leader and people voice each petition in a shared, dialogical fashion (Form F). Many prayers include designated spaces where the people may pray silently or aloud (Forms, E, F, I).

A popular approach to congregational involvement is the litany form in which people respond to each petition with a short response or acclamation. While such responses should remain the same throughout a given prayer, they may vary from Sunday to Sunday as a way to claim congregational attention and to enrich the spirit of the prayer.

In the responsorial prayer (Form C), the author offers three different congregational responses. These brief exclamations are taken from the Opening Prayers and Psalms of the Roman rite and readily answer the leader's "We pray to the Lord." The leader might end each intercession with "Lord, in your mercy." Alternate congregational responses include:

Hear our prayer.

Show us your saving power.

Bless your people with peace.

Reveal your power.

Let your face shine upon us.

Strengthen us with your Holy Spirit.

Give your people joy and peace.

Following a long tradition in the church, occasionally the Greek *Kyrie eleison* ("Lord, have mercy") might be used as a response to the intercessions.

Just as the Hebrew "Amen" and "Alleluia" were carried over into the services of the Greek-speaking Jews, so the Greek *Kyrie* was continued in the later Latin and other vernacular services in the West. This unity of thought amid diversity of language suggests the "one church" and the "one Lord, one faith, one Baptism" of which St. Paul speaks. Since it corresponds to universal need and universal faith, the simple cry of the *Kyrie* has sounded in many forms in all eras.[5]

Not only do these repeated responses insure congregational involvement, but they also provide a stable rhythm for the prayers. Repetition in any ritual exercise is a positive value which makes things memorable and fuses people together in common purpose. It is conceivable that such refrains might be meaningful not only during the prayer, but also as a memorable phrase for the day or week.

There are other ways of involving the people in prayer refrains. The verses of a familiar hymn might be alternated with the petitions of the prayer. If this combination of hymn and prayer is to succeed, the tune must be a familar one, and the words of the hymn must be appropriate to the text of the prayer.

The Language of Prayer

Romano Guardini once said: "For the sake of speech we must practice silence."[6] Practicing silence may be a positive first step in addressing our present predicament with words. We are a people inundated by words. Words are broadcasted at us, stacked by millions in micro-chips, their broken shapes scattered across our landscapes. Like so much graffiti, words cover the floor, the walls, and the ceilings of our existence.

One reason for the present crisis in preaching is a lost confidence in words. Words are cheap, disposable things. We have learned to endure the onslaught of words in the same semi-conscious state in which we listen to Muzak. We carry this disposition, this inability to attentively listen, into Christian worship, where we are also bombarded by words. Our spirits cry out for silence, for "actions that speak louder than words," for a few chosen words spoken with care and economy. Instead we come away from most worship experiences with our communication systems jammed by a preponderance of words.

Liturgically, silence is golden because it reminds us that the first business of Christian life is listening to God. "In the beginning was the Word"—that is not only the opening of the Gospel of St. John, but also of Christian faith and life. We cannot speak or act with integrity until we have heard and deeply pondered God's word to us. Silence is the sign of a relationship that is simply "beyond words."

So often stereotyped as an inward, personal experience, silence is a unifying agent in the gathered assembly. As we surrender our preoccupation with words, we grow in sensitivity to those around us. We listen to the lives of our neighbors. Intercession is essentially first a matter of being with others in the name of Christ, then it is "mentioning others" in prayer.

Silence should be an ingredient in the spiritual discipline of the intercessor, and it should be essential to his or her public prayer. Most examples of prayer in this book promote intentional periods of silence within the prayer of the faithful. Keeping silence in prayer is a skill that must be learned and tested in each local congregation. The invitation-silence-collecting prayer format embraces a style of guided silence.

If the people are unpracticed in the use of silence, this prompting through brief evocative bids will lead them to a deeper appreciation of its ministry.

A word that comes forth from silence is a word with power. When the worshiping assembly keeps silence in prayer, their expectancy is nourished and so is their participation in the words that finally emerge. Furthermore, it is generally believed that words that come out of silence are well-considered thoughts, worthy of our attention and respect. We tend to listen more carefully to such words. "For the sake of speech we must practice silence."

In the spirit of public prayer we use words with great economy. A rambling, undisciplined prayer or a long monolog is an offense to the people gathered to pray. The congregation cannot give interior assent to prayers that are too long or complex for immediate understanding. Simple, direct expression spoken deliberately allows people to grasp and own the words of the leader. In the end such brevity is a recognition of the democracy of public prayer, of the necessary reciprocity between leader and people.

When Luther cut back the enormous growth of the Medieval Mass, his pastoral instincts led him to simplify forms of prayer and song. In limiting the lengthy gradual to two verses, he suggested that those interested could sing the other verses at home. In what might serve as a good rule for liturgical prayer, he wrote: "In church we do not want to quench the spirit of the faithful with tedium."[7] In this age of billboard slogans and 60-second commercials our attention span is short, and those who lead us in worship need to appreciate this cultural handicap.

The prayer of the faithful should be guided by a sense of classic restraint. Petitions that are preachy or overly didactic fail in the assembly because they are felt to be manipulative. Cute or ingenious expressions call attention to the cleverness of the prayer leader and disable the ability of a group to pray. If we must pause to consider an interesting twist in the language, we have already lost something of the force of our intention to pray. Restraint would ask for language that has one primary function: to aid common prayer.

The historic collect has been a much admired form of prayer in the Western stream of liturgy. Coming from early Medieval sources and reshaped by the literary genius of such people as Thomas Cranmer, the collect has served as a centerpiece for any discussion of public prayer language. The Collect for Purity from the gathering rite of the American *Book of Common Prayer* is a worthy example.

> Almighty God, to you all hearts are open, all desires known, and from you no secrets are hid: Cleanse the thoughts of our hearts by the inspiration of your Holy Spirit, that we may perfectly love you, and worthily magnify your holy Name; through Christ our Lord. Amen.[8]

This is, writes Daniel Stevick, an "unusually happy marriage of sense and form."[9] Like its Latin original, this prayer is a single sentence, its wording compact and concise. It follows a traditional fivefold form which in outline might be stated:

address to God,
an attribute of God (antecedent reason as ground for prayer)
the petition
hoped-for consequence
ending ("through Jesus Christ our Lord")[10]

Such prayer is often winsome because of the rhythmic weaving of its parts and the poetic shaping of its words. Clarity, brevity, restraint characterize this and other collects that have come to be cherished in Christian worship.

The prayer of the faithful may indeed be a series of such collects chosen from various sources to reflect the concerns of a given Sunday. Each may end with the phrase "through Jesus Christ our Lord," and the congregation may add their "Amen" after each petition. The *Lutheran Book of Worship* provides a collection of such prayers (pages 42-53). *Occasional Services* gives a complete topical index of every collect in both *Lutheran Book of Worship* and *Occasional Services*.[11] The *Book of Common Prayer* provides a similar book of prayers.[12] This is indexed by Marion J. Hatchett in his *Commentary on the American Prayer Book*.

It should be noted that such prayers have sometimes been criticized as too cerebral and almost too perfect in construction. We may admire their well-balanced construction and majestic rhythm much as we appreciate a work of art; however, they do not always elicit the genuine feelings of the people. Elevated language, certainly appropriate to public worship, must at times give way to the immediate and everyday.[13]

These collects are an example of prayer that does not equivocate, for at their center is a vocative, straightforward beseeching of God in prayer. An unfortunate characteristic of one of the collections of prayers noted (see Form C) is the weakness of many of the petitions that begin with the polite word "may." "May this city not be forsaken" rendered in the vocative mode would be "Forsake not this city." Form D in this chapter begins every petition with the imperative—grant, guide, give, bless, comfort, and heal. Our prayers should not be a kind of wishful thinking in God's presence, but an urgent asking after God.

"Talk of God is always indirect."[14] In prayer, as in hymn and homily, we speak of God in terms of things that are like God. We refer to God as shepherd, lamb, rock, bread, bridegroom. This pervasive use of metaphors in liturgy addresses

One who cannot be captured by speech, thought, or action. The ultimate purpose of liturgical language is neither to impress nor to instruct, but to signal the transcendent Other, the God who stubbornly refuses to submit to any of our categories—whether of name, time, number, or gender.[15]

Religious language is full of images. Metaphor, a characteristic in prayer-speech, provides part of the answer to the need for inclusive language. By now, we have firm evidence of the heavy use of masculine pronouns and masculine images of God as Father, Lord, and King in biblical and liturgical language. Using only such terms not only excludes half of the congregation through linguistic sexism, but it also robs all of us of the richness of other metaphors. We need fresh, creative attempts at the kind of relational metaphors that will more fully touch the lives of the whole people of God. An unusually good example of a feminine image in prayer comes from a collect for sending forth of communion ministers in Distribution of Communion to Those in Special Circumstances (*Occasional Services*):

Gracious God, loving all your family with a mother's tender care: As you sent the angel to feed Elijah with heavenly bread, assist us in this ministry on which we set forth. In your love and care, nourish and strengthen those to whom we bring this Sacrament, that through the body and blood of your Son we all may know the comfort of your abiding presence. Amen.[16]

Another characteristic of metaphor in prayer-speech is the use of transformational images. Such prayer does not accept the status quo. God has acted decisively in our lives and we gladly rehearse the story. Freed from the bondage of the old order of sin and death, in intercession we anticipate the blessings and renewal of all creation. The following prayer is rich in transformational content:

Gracious Lord of all, we your people rejoice at the wonder of our deliverance from bondage to freedom, from agony to joy, from mourning to festivity, from darkness to light, and from servitude to redemption. In all our words and ways we would praise you for the surpassing goodness that fills all time and space; for the life, death, and resurrection of your Son, our Savior; and for sending the Spirit to lead us into his eternal peace. As we have been bountifully blessed, make us a blessing to your world.[17]

One of the most powerful references in Christian prayer is the use of scriptural images. A single word, a place, or person's name can call forth the great common stories that give identity and direction to the community. When the concerns of our present life are placed next to these salvation stories, the product is a powerful expression of prayer. A prayer for travelers in the *Lutheran Book of Worship* is an excellent example:

Lord God our Father, you kept Abraham and Sarah in safety throughout the days of their pilgrimage, you led the children of Israel through the midst of the sea, and by a star you led the Wise Men to the infant Jesus. Protect and guide us now in this time as we set out to travel, make our ways safe and our homecomings joyful, and bring us at last to our heavenly home, where you dwell in glory with your Son and the Holy Spirit, God forever. Amen.[18]

Our progress in this section has been from silence to speech, and now, to song. Before liturgy was a text to be read, the words of the rite were the libretto for the people's song. Sung prayer, so common to our forebearers, deserves to be considered a desirable alternative. Sung litanies (Form J) and hymn prayers are included in most worship texts, and, with careful introduction, they could become a valued part of the congregation's repertoire. Song remembers the ecstatic roots of all human speech. Song is celebrative and, therefore, an ideal mode of Christian communication. Sung prayer, although pre-cast, has the power to engage and involve us when spoken words do not.

Various Models of Intercessory Prayer

The *Book of Common Prayer* has been a rich resource for the whole family of English-speaking liturgies. With foresight, the framers of the 1979 American edition provided examples of intercessory prayer for those called to lead the Prayers of the People. They are presented here to show something of the variety possible in form and language of the prayers. and to prompt those who share in this ministry.

Form D is an example of an adaptation of ancient litanies of the Eastern Orthodox Church. Depending on local decision, certain paragraphs are omitted and space is provided for the inclusion of contemporary concerns. A brief pause should be kept before the response "Lord, have mercy." Form E makes use of directed silence as the intercessor says, "Pray for justice and peace." A simple, helpful form is provided here for extemporary prayers and petitions. Form F, a revised prayer from the Church of New Zealand, is an example of a short dialogical or responsorial prayer. Form G follows a pattern of intention–collect–prayer–silence–response. Form H is based on a modern Spanish litany from Easter sources in which each petition includes the reason for which that prayer is made. Form I is a combination of themes, beginning as a responsive prayer, moving to a broad extemporaneous section, and then ending with a unison confessional prayer.

An example of a sung litany (Form J) is borrowed from the liturgy of Evening Prayer in the *Lutheran Book of Worship*.

Finally in this chapter four examples are printed from a valuable resource, *The Wideness of God's Mercy*, prayers gathered and edited by Jeffery Rowthorn.[19] Form K is a short morning litany from the ecumenical community of Taize, France. Form L, while not strictly an intercessory prayer, shows a lively complement of psalm verse and hymn stanza. An original prayer by Lucien Deiss, Form M, is a lovely Christmas litany of birth. The inclusive language of Form N is reflected in the antiphonal voicing of the petitions by both women and men.

All prefabricated prayers must be used prudently and, as stated, are no substitute for the indigenous shaping of prayers by the local agent of the assembly.

Concluding Prayer

The presiding minister often concludes the prayers with a short collect such as: "Into your hands, O Lord, we commend all for whom we pray, trusting in your mercy; through your Son, Jesus Christ our Lord."

Like the introductory address, this conclusion could be varied. Examples of other concluding collects are printed on page 73.

Appendix

Form A

Prayer of the Church

A Almighty God, giver of all things, with gladness we give thanks for all your goodness. We bless you for the love which has created and which sustains us from day to day. We praise you for the gift of your Son our Savior, through whom you have made known your will and grace. We thank you for the Holy Spirit, the comforter; for your holy church; for the means of grace; for the lives of all faithful and good people; and for the hope of the life to come. Help us to treasure in our hearts all that our Lord has done for us, and enable us to show our thankfulness by lives that are wholly given to your service.

C **Hear us, good Lord.**

A Save and defend your whole church, purchased with the precious blood of Christ. Give it pastors and ministers filled with your Spirit, and strengthen it through the Word and the holy sacraments. Make it perfect in love and in all good works, and establish it in the faith delivered to the saints. Sanctify and unite your people in all the world, that one holy church may bear witness to you, the creator and redeemer of all.

C **Hear us, good Lord.**

A Give your wisdom and heavenly grace to all pastors and to those who hold office in your church, that, by their faithful service, faith may abound and your kingdom increase.

C **Hear us, good Lord.**

A Send the light of your truth into all the earth. Raise up faithful servants of Christ to labor in the gospel both at home and in distant lands.

C **Hear us, good Lord.**

A In your mercy strengthen the younger churches and support them in times of trial. Make them steadfast, abounding in the work of the Lord, and let their faith and zeal for the gospel refresh and renew the witness of your people everywhere.

C **Hear us, good Lord.**

Ⓐ Preserve our nation in justice and honor, that we may lead a peaceable life of integrity. Grant health and favor to all who bear office in our land

(Canada) *especially to Her Gracious Majesty, the Queen; the Governor General; the Prime Minister and the Parliament; the government of this province and all who have authority over us*

(USA) *especially to the president of the United States, the governor of this state, and all those who make, administer, and judge our laws*

and help them to serve this people according to your holy will.

Ⓒ **Hear us, good Lord.**

Ⓐ Take from us all hatred and prejudice, give us the spirit of love, and dispose our days in your peace. Prosper the labors of those who take counsel for the nations of the world, that mutual understanding and common endeavor may be increased among all peoples.

Ⓒ **Hear us, good Lord.**

Ⓐ Bless the schools of the church and all colleges, universities, and centers of research and those who teach in them. Bestow your wisdom in such measure that people may serve you in church and state and that our common life may be conformed to the rule of your truth and justice.

Ⓒ **Hear us, good Lord.**

Ⓐ Sanctify our homes with your presence and joy. Keep our children in the covenant of their baptism and enable their parents to rear them in a life of faith and devotion. By the spirit of affection and service unite the members of all families, that they may show your praise in our land and in all the world.

Ⓒ **Hear us, good Lord.**

Ⓐ Let your blessing rest upon the seedtime and harvest, the commerce and industry, the leisure and rest, the arts and culture of our people. Take under your special protection those whose work is difficult or dangerous, and be with all who lay their hands to any useful task. Give them just rewards for their labor and the knowledge that their work is good in your sight.

Ⓒ **Hear us, good Lord.**

Special supplications, intercessions, and thanksgivings may be made.

Ⓐ Comfort with the grace of your Holy Spirit all who are in sorrow or need, sickness or adversity. Remember those who suffer persecution for the faith. Have mercy on those to whom death draws near. Bring consolation to those in sorrow or mourning. And to all grant a measure of your love, taking them into your tender care.

Ⓒ **Hear us, good Lord.**

Ⓐ We remember with thanksgiving those who have loved and served you in your church on earth, who now rest from their labors [especially those most dear to us, whom we name in our hearts before you]. Keep us in fellowship with all your saints, and bring us at last to the joy of your heavenly kingdom.

Ⓒ **Hear us, good Lord.**

Ⓐ All these things and whatever else you see that we need, grant us, Father, for the sake of him who died and rose again, and now lives and reigns with you in the unity of the Holy Spirit, one God forever.

Ⓒ **Amen**

Form B

Bidding Prayer

Ⓐ Let us pray, brothers and sisters, for the holy church of God throughout the world, that God the almighty Father guide it and gather it together, so that we may worship him in peace and tranquility.

Silent prayer.

Ⓟ Almighty and eternal God, you have shown your glory to all nations in Jesus Christ. Guide the work of the church. Help it to persevere in faith, proclaim your name, and bring salvation to people everywhere. We ask this through Christ our Lord.

Ⓒ **Amen.**

Ⓐ Let us pray for _____ name _____ and _____ name _____, for our pastors and other ministers, for all servants of the church, and for all the people of God.

Silent prayer.

Ⓟ Almighty and eternal God, your Spirit guides the church and makes it holy. Strengthen and uphold our pastors and our leaders; keep them in health and safety for the good of the church, and help each of us to do faithfully the work to which you have called us. We ask this through Christ our Lord.

Ⓒ **Amen.**

Ⓐ Let us pray for those preparing for Baptism, that God make them responsive to his love and give them new life in Jesus Christ.

Silent prayer.

Ⓟ Almighty and eternal God, you continually bless the church with new members. Increase the faith and understanding of those preparing for Baptism. Give them a new birth as your children, and keep them in the faith and communion of your holy church. We ask this through Christ our Lord.

Ⓒ **Amen.**

Ⓐ Let us pray for all our brothers and sisters who share our faith in Jesus Christ, that God may gather and keep together in one church all those who know Christ as Lord.

Silent prayer.

P Almighty and eternal God, you give your church its unity. Look with favor on all who follow Jesus your Son. We are all consecrated to you by our Baptism; make us one in the fullness of faith, and keep us one in the fellowship of love. We ask this through Christ our Lord.

C **Amen.**

A Let us pray for the Jewish people, the first to hear the Word of God, that they may receive the fulfillment of the covenant's promises.

Silent prayer.

P Almighty and eternal God, long ago you gave your promise to Abraham and his posterity. Hear the prayers of your church that the people you first made your own may arrive with us at the fullness of redemption. We ask this through Christ our Lord.

C **Amen.**

A Let us pray for those who do not believe in Christ, that the light of the Holy Spirit may show them the way of salvation.

Silent prayer.

P Almighty and eternal God, enable those who do not acknowledge Christ to receive the truth of the gospel. Help us, your people, to grow in love for one another, to grasp more fully the mystery of your Godhead, and so to become more perfect witnesses of your love in the sight of all people. We ask this through Christ our Lord.

C **Amen.**

A Let us pray for those who do not believe in God, that they may find him who is the author and goal of our existence.

Silent prayer.

P Almighty and eternal God, you created humanity so that all might long to know you and have peace in you. Grant that, in spite of the hurtful things that stand in their way, they may all recognize in the lives of Christians the tokens of your love and mercy, and gladly acknowledge you as the one true God and Father of us all. We ask this through Christ our Lord.

C **Amen.**

A Let us pray for those who serve in public office, that God may guide their minds and hearts, so that all of us may live in true peace and freedom.

Silent prayer.

P Almighty and eternal God, you are the champion of the poor and oppressed. In your goodness, watch over those in authority, so that people everywhere may enjoy justice, peace, freedom, and a share in the goodness of your creation. We ask this through Christ our Lord.

C Amen.

A Let us pray that God, the almighty and merciful Father, may heal the sick, comfort the dying, give safety to travelers, free those unjustly deprived of liberty, and rid the world of falsehood, hunger, and disease.

Silent prayer.

P Almighty and eternal God, you give strength to the weary and new courage to those who have lost heart. Hear the prayers of all who call on you in any trouble, that they may have the joy of receiving your help in their need. We ask this through Christ our Lord.

C Amen.

A Finally, let us pray for all those things for which our Lord would have us ask.

C **Our Father in heaven,**
   hallowed be your name,
   your kingdom come,
   your will be done,
      on earth as in heaven.
Give us today our daily bread.
Forgive us our sins
   as we forgive those
      who sin against us.
Save us from the time of trial
   and deliver us from evil.
For the kingdom, the power, and
   the glory are yours, now and
   forever. Amen

OR

C **Our Father who art in heaven,**
   hallowed be thy name,
   thy kingdom come,
   thy will be done,
      on earth as it is in heaven.
Give us this day our daily bread;
and forgive us our trespasses,
   as we forgive
      those who trespass against us;
and lead us not into temptation,
   but deliver us from evil.
For thine is the kingdom, and
   the power, and the glory,
   forever and ever. Amen.

Form C

The Feast of the Epiphany (A, B, and C)

The response to the intercessions is:
    Lead us to glory (in heaven).
or **May your love be near.**
or **Every nation adores you.**

Ⓐ Let us pray for the church:

Silence for prayer

God, whose promise is for all nations;
Sustain the Christmas glory still.
May the Lord shine upon us.
By the Holy Spirit, reveal your plan.
We pray to the Lord:

Ⓒ **Lead us to glory.**

Ⓐ Let us pray for God's light:

Silence for prayer

May the nations walk by your light
And kings and queens by your shining radiance.
Let all search together for profound peace.
We pray to the Lord:

Ⓒ **Lead us to glory.**

Ⓐ Let us pray for those without strength:

Silence for prayer

Save the lives of the poor.
Rescue them when they cry out.
Govern your people with justice
And your afflicted ones with careful judgment.
We pray to the Lord:

Ⓒ **Lead us to glory.**

Ⓐ Let us pray for unity among all believers:

Silence for prayer

Bring the new epiphany
Where all will share the promise and rise in splendor.
In the Spirit all
Are called to love.
We pray to the Lord:

C **Lead us to glory.**

A Let us pray for all travelers:

Silence for prayer

May those who study the heavens follow the star
To the place where Christ is
And there, like the Magi, do him homage.
Reveal your plan by the Holy Spirit.
We pray to the Lord:

C **Lead us to glory.**

A Let us remember the dead:

Silence for prayer

May the Beloved rise in splendor.
Banish the darkness that covers the earth.
Let glory appear.
We pray to the Lord:

C **Lead us to glory.**

Form D

🅐 With all our heart and with all our mind, let us pray to the Lord, saying, "Lord, have mercy."

🅐 For the peace from above, for the loving kindness of God, and for the salvation of our souls, let us pray to the Lord.

🅒 **Lord, have mercy.**

🅐 For the peace of the world, for the welfare of the holy church of God, and for the unity of all peoples, let us pray to the Lord.

🅒 **Lord, have mercy.**

🅐 For our bishop, and for all the clergy and people, let us pray to the Lord.

🅒 **Lord, have mercy.**

🅐 For our president, for the leaders of the nations, and for all in authority, let us pray to the Lord.

🅒 **Lord, have mercy.**

🅐 For this city (town, village, _____), for every city and community, and for those who live in them, let us pray to the Lord.

🅒 **Lord, have mercy.**

🅐 For seasonable weather, and for an abundance of the fruits of the earth, let us pray to the Lord.

🅒 **Lord, have mercy.**

🅐 For the good earth which God has given us, and for the wisdom and will to conserve it, let us pray to the Lord.

🅒 **Lord, have mercy.**

🅐 For those who travel on land, on water, or in the air [or through outer space], let us pray to the Lord.

🅒 **Lord, have mercy.**

🅐 For the aged and infirm, for the widowed and orphans, and for the sick and the suffering, let us pray to the Lord.

🅒 **Lord, have mercy.**

Ⓐ For _____ , let us pray to the Lord.

Ⓒ **Lord, have mercy.**

Ⓐ For the poor and the oppressed, for the unemployed and the destitute, for prisoners and captives, and for all who remember and care for them, let us pray to the Lord.

Ⓒ **Lord, have mercy.**

Ⓐ For all who have died in the hope of the resurrection, and for all the departed, let us pray to the Lord.

Ⓒ **Lord, have mercy.**

Ⓐ For deliverance from all danger, violence, oppression, and degradation, let us pray to the Lord.

Ⓒ **Lord, have mercy.**

Ⓐ For the absolution and remission of our sins and offenses, let us pray to the Lord.

Ⓒ **Lord, have mercy.**

Ⓐ That we may end our lives in faith and hope, without suffering and without reproach, let us pray to the Lord.

Ⓒ **Lord, have mercy.**

Ⓐ Defend us, deliver us, and in thy compassion protect us, O Lord, by thy grace.

Ⓒ **Lord, have mercy.**

Ⓐ In the communion of [_____ and of all the] saints, let us commend ourselves, and one another, and all our life, to Christ our God.

Ⓒ **To thee, O Lord our God.**

Silence

The celebrant adds a concluding collect.

Form E

In the course of the silence after each bidding, the people offer their own prayers, either silently or aloud.

A I ask your prayers for God's people throughout the world; for our bishop(s) ~~Herbert~~ / Ralph _____ ; for this gathering; and for all ministers and people.
Pray for the church.

Silence

A I ask your prayers for peace, for goodwill among nations, and for the well-being of all people.
Pray for justice and peace.

Silence

A I ask your prayers for the poor, the sick, the hungry, the oppressed, and those in prison.
Pray for those in any need or trouble.

Silence

A I ask your prayers for all who seek God or a deeper knowledge of him.
Pray that they may find and be found by him.

Silence

A I ask your prayers for the departed [especially _____].
Pray for those who have died.

Silence

Members of the congregation may ask the prayers or the thanksgiving of those present: I ask now for any other prayers of concern or thanks
I ask your prayers for _____ . which you would hopefully
I ask your thanksgiving for _____ . and faithfully share with
this community of prayer

Silence

A Praise God for those in every generation in whom Christ has been honored [especially _____ whom we remember today].
Pray that we may have grace to glorify Christ in our own day.

some of the first missionaries to China & Asia

Francis Xavier
S.J.
Japan 1549
Robert Morrison, China 1807
1st Prot
Karl Guetzlaff, 1st Luth to China
Hudson Taylor 1854

Silence

The celebrant adds a concluding collect.

56

Form F

The leader and people pray responsively.

Ⓐ Father, we pray for your holy catholic church;

Ⓒ That we all may be one.

Ⓐ Grant that every member of the church may truly and humbly serve you;

Ⓒ That your name may be glorified by all people.

Ⓐ We pray for all bishops, priests, and deacons;

Ⓒ That they may be faithful ministers of your Word and sacraments.

Ⓐ We pray for all who govern and hold authority in the nations of the world;

Ⓒ That there may be justice and peace on the earth.

Ⓐ Give us grace to do your will in all that we undertake;

Ⓒ That our works may find favor in your sight.

Ⓐ Have compassion on those who suffer from any grief or trouble;

Ⓒ That they may be delivered from their distress.

Ⓐ Give to the departed eternal rest;

Ⓒ Let light perpetual shine upon them.

Ⓐ We praise you for your saints who have entered into joy;

Ⓒ May we also come to share in your heavenly kingdom.

Ⓐ Let us pray for our own needs and those of others.

Silence

The people may add their own petitions.
The celebrant adds a concluding collect.

Form G

Ⓐ Let us pray for the church and for the world.

Ⓐ Grant, Almighty God, that all who confess your name may be united in your truth, live together in your love, and reveal your glory in the world.

Silence

Ⓐ Lord, in your mercy

Ⓒ **Hear our prayer.**

Ⓐ Guide the people of this land and of all the nations in the ways of justice and peace, that we may honor one another and serve the common good.

Silence

Ⓐ Lord, in your mercy

Ⓒ **Hear our prayer.**

Ⓐ Give us all a reverence for the earth as your own creation, that we may use its resources rightly in the service of others and to your honor and glory.

Silence

Ⓐ Lord, in your mercy

Ⓒ **Hear our prayer.**

Ⓐ Bless all whose lives are closely linked with ours, and grant that we may serve Christ in them, and love one another as he loves us.

Silence

Ⓐ Lord, in your mercy

Ⓒ **Hear our prayer.**

Ⓐ Comfort and heal all those who suffer in body, mind, or spirit; give them courage and hope in their troubles, and bring them the joy of salvation.

Silence

Ⓐ Lord, in your mercy

Ⓒ **Hear our prayer.**

Ⓐ We commend to your mercy all who have died, that your will for them may be fulfilled; and we pray that we may share with all your saints in your eternal kingdom.

Silence

Ⓐ Lord, in your mercy

Ⓒ **Hear our prayer.**

The celebrant adds a concluding collect.

Form H

Ⓐ In peace, let us pray to the Lord, saying "Lord, have mercy" (*or* "Kyrie eleison").

Ⓐ For the holy church of God, that it may be filled with truth and love, and be found without fault at the day of your coming, we pray to you, O Lord.

Here and after every petition the people respond

Kyrie eleison. *or* **Lord, have mercy.**

Ⓐ For *N.* our presiding bishop, for *N. (N.)* our own bishop(s), for all bishops and other ministers, and for all the holy people of God, we pray to you, O Lord.

Ⓐ For all who fear God and believe in you, Lord Christ, that our divisions may cease, and that all may be one as you and the Father are one, we pray to you, O Lord.

Ⓐ For the mission of the church, that in faithful witness it may preach the gospel to the ends of the earth, we pray to you, O Lord.

Ⓐ For those who do not yet believe, and for those who have lost their faith, that they may receive the light of the Gospel, we pray to you, O Lord.

Ⓐ For the peace of the world, that a spirit of respect and forbearance may grow among nations and peoples, we pray to you, O Lord.

Ⓐ For those in positions of public trust [especially _____], that they may serve justice, and promote the dignity and freedom of every person, we pray to you, O Lord.

Ⓐ For all who live and work in this community [especially _____], we pray to you, O Lord.

Ⓐ For a blessing upon all human labor, and for the right use of the riches of creation, that the world may be freed from poverty, famine, and disaster, we pray to you, O Lord.

Ⓐ For the poor, the persecuted, the sick, and all who suffer; for refugees, prisoners, and all who are in danger; that they may be relieved and protected, we pray to you, O Lord.

Ⓐ For this congregation [for those who are present, and for those who are absent], that we may be delivered from hardness of heart, and show forth your glory in all that we do, we pray to you, O Lord.

Ⓐ For our enemies and those who wish us harm; and for all whom we have injured or offended, we pray to you, O Lord.

Ⓐ For ourselves; for the forgiveness of our sins, and for the grace of the Holy Spirit to amend our lives, we pray to you, O Lord.

Ⓐ For all who have commended themselves to our prayers; for our families, friends, and neighbors; that being freed from anxiety, they may live in joy, peace, and health, we pray to you, O Lord.

Ⓐ For _____ , we pray to you, O Lord.

Ⓐ For all who have died in the communion of your church, and those whose faith is known to you alone, that, with all the saints, they may have rest in that place where there is no pain or grief, but life eternal, we pray to you, O Lord.

Ⓐ Rejoicing in the fellowship of [the ever-blessed Virgin Mary, *(blessed N.)* and] all the saints, let us commend ourselves, and one another, and all our life to Christ our God.

Ⓒ **To you, O Lord our God.**

Silence

The celebrant adds a concluding collect or the following doxology.

Ⓐ For yours is the majesty, O Father, Son, and Holy Spirit; yours is the kingdom and the power and the glory, now and forever. Amen.

Form I

The leader and people pray responsively.

A In peace, we pray to you, Lord God.

Silence

A For all people in their daily life and work;

C **For our families, friends, and neighbors, and for those who are alone.**

A For this community, the nation, and the world;

C **For all who work for justice, freedom, and peace.**

A For the just and proper use of your creation;

C **For the victims of hunger, fear, injustice, and oppression.**

A For all who are in danger, sorrow, or any kind of trouble;

C **For those who minister to the sick, the friendless, and the needy.**

A For the peace and unity of the church of God;

C **For all who proclaim the gospel and all who seek the truth.**

A For [*N.* our presiding bishop, and *N. (N.)* our bishop(s); and for] all bishops and other ministers;

C **For all who serve God in his church.**

A For the special needs and concerns of this congregation.

Silence

The people may add their own petitions.

A Hear us, Lord;

C **For your mercy is great.**

A We thank you, Lord, for all the blessings of this life.

Silence

The people may add their own thanksgivings.

A We will exalt you, O God our King;

C **And praise your name for ever and ever.**

A We pray for all who have died, that they may have a place in your eternal kingdom.

Silence

The people may add their own petitions.

A Lord, let your loving-kindness be upon them;

C **Who put their trust in you.**

A We pray to you also for the forgiveness of our sins.

Silence may be kept.

C **Have mercy upon us, most merciful Father;**
in your compassion forgive us our sins,
known and unknown,
things done and left undone;
and so uphold us by your Spirit
that we may live and serve you in newness of life,
to the honor and glory of your name;
through Jesus Christ our Lord. Amen.

The celebrant concludes with an absolution or a suitable collect.

Form J

The LITANY is sung or said. The complete Litany may be sung to the alternate musical form.

L In peace, let us pray to the Lord.

C Lord, have mer - cy.

L In peace, let us pray to the Lord.

C Lord, have mer - cy.

L For the peace from above, and for our salvation, let us pray to the Lord.

C Lord, have mer - cy.

L For the peace of the whole world, for the well-being
of the Church of God, and for the unity of all, let us pray. . . to the Lord.

C Lord, have mer - cy.

L For this holy house, and for all who offer
here their worship and praise, let us pray . . . . to the Lord.

C Lord, have mer - cy.

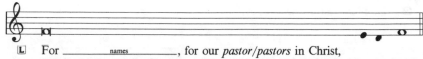

L For _____ names _____, for our *pastor/pastors* in Christ,
for all servants of the Church, and for all the people, let us pray to the Lord.

C Lord, have mer - cy.

L For our public servants, for the government
and those who protect us, that they may be
upheld and strengthened in every good deed, let us pray . . to the Lord.

C Lord, have mer - cy.

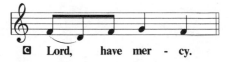

L For those who work to bring peace, justice, health,
and protection in this and every place, let us pray . . . . to the Lord.

C Lord, have mer - cy.

L For those who bring offerings, those
who do good works in this congregation,
those who toil, those who sing, and
all the people here present who await
from the Lord great and abundant mercy, let us pray · · · to the Lord.

C Lord, have mer - cy.

L For favorable weather, for an abundance of the fruits
of the earth, and for peaceful times, let us pray · · · · · to the Lord.

C Lord, have mer - cy.

L For our deliverance from all affliction,
wrath, danger, and need, let us pray · · · · · · · · · to the Lord.

C Lord, have mer - cy.

L For the faithful who have gone
before us and are at rest, let us give thanks · · · · · · · to the Lord.

C Al - le - lu - ia.

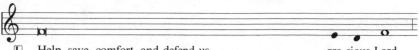

L   Help, save, comfort, and defend us, ... gra-cious Lord.

Silence for meditation

L   Rejoicing in the fellowship of all the saints, let us
commend ourselves, one another, and our whole life to Christ, our Lord.

C   To   you, O   Lord.

L O God, from whom come all holy desires, all good counsels, and all just works:
Give to us, your servants, that peace which the world cannot give, that our hearts may
be set to obey your commandments; and also that we, being defended from the fear
of our enemies, may live in peace and quietness; through the merits of Jesus Christ
our Savior, who lives and reigns with you and the Holy Spirit, God forever.

C Amen

Form K

A God, our Creator, you are the maker of heaven and earth:

C **Be our freedom, Lord!**

A God, our Savior, you redeem us all:

C **Be our freedom, Lord!**

A God, Holy Spirit, you sanctify our lives:

C **Be our freedom, Lord!**

A By your incarnation and your birth in poverty, by your baptism, your fasting, and your trials in the desert:

C **Be our freedom, Lord!**

A By your agony in the garden, by your cross and passion, by your death and burial, by your resurrection and ascension, and by the gifts of your Holy Spirit:

C **Be our freedom, Lord!**

A In times of trouble, and when all goes well, at the hour we die, and on the day of your glory:

C **Be our freedom, Lord!**

A From war and violence, from hardness of heart and from contempt of your love and your promises:

C **Be our freedom, Lord!**

A Enlighten this day with your word, that in it we may find our way and our hope:

C **Be our freedom, Lord!**

A Assist your people in every land, govern them in peace and justice, defend them from the enemies of life:

C **Be our freedom, Lord!**

Form L

[I] Alleluia!
Sing to the Lord a new song;
sing God's praise in the congregation of the faithful.

[II] Let Israel rejoice in its maker;
let the children of Zion be joyful in their king.

C When in our music God is glorified,
and adoration leaves no room for pride,
it is as though the whole creation cried:
Alleluia!

[I] Let them praise God's name in the dance;
let them sing praise to God with timbrel and harp.

[II] For the Lord takes pleasure in his people
and adorns the poor with victory.

C How often, making music, we have found
a new dimension in the world of sound,
as worship moved us to a more profound
Alleluia!

[I] Alleluia!
Praise God in his holy temple;
praise God in the firmament of his power.

[II] Praise God for his mighty acts;
praise God for his excellent greatness.

C So has the church, in liturgy and song,
in faith and love, through centuries of wrong,
borne witness to the truth in ev'ry tongue:
Alleluia!

[I] Praise God with the blast of the ram's horn;
praise God with lyre and harp.

[II] Praise God with timbrel and dance;
praise God with strings and pipe.

C And did not Jesus sing a psalm that night
when utmost evil strove against the light?
Then let us sing, for whom he won the fight:
Alleluia!

[I] Praise God with resounding cymbals;
praise God with loud-clanging cymbals.

[II] Let everything that has breath praise the Lord.
Alleluia!

C Let ev'ry instrument be tuned for praise;
let all rejoice who have a voice to raise;
and may God give us faith to sing always:
Alleluia!

Form M

I For all who give you a face, Lord Jesus,

II by spreading your love in the world:

C We praise you.

I For all who give you hands, Lord Jesus,

II by doing their best toward their brothers and sisters:

C We praise you.

I For all who give you a mouth, Lord Jesus,

II by defending the weak and the oppressed:

C We praise you.

I For all who give you eyes, Lord Jesus,

II by seeing every bit of love in the heart of man and woman:

C We praise you.

I For all who give you a heart, Lord Jesus,

II by preferring the poor to the rich, the weak to the strong:

C We praise you.

I For all who give to your poverty, Lord Jesus,

II the look of hope for the Kingdom:

C We praise you.

I For all who reveal you simply by what they are, Lord Jesus,

II because they reflect your beauty in their lives:

C We praise you.

I God our Father, you are the God of a thousand faces,

II yet nothing can reveal you completely except the face of the child of Bethlehem:

**C We pray to you:
Continue in our lives the mystery of Christmas.
Let your Son become flesh in us
so that we may be for all our brothers and sisters
the revelation of your ever-present love. Amen.**

Form N

Leader: Let us not falter in hope! Let us offer our praise and our lives to the Lord.

Men: God of the patriarchs,

Women: God of the matriarchs,

All: In line with all your faithful people in every age, we offer ourselves and our gifts for the service of your kingdom!

Women: God of Abraham, Isaac, and Jacob,

Men: God of Sarah, Rebekah, and Rachel,

All: Grant us the courage to cling to your promise, even if all the world seems hostile and our own hearts judge us failures.

Men: God of Priscilla and Aquila,

Women: God of Moses and of Miriam,

All: May we, too, labor in harmony to bring our people out of bondage and darkness.

Women: O God of Deborah, a mother in Israel,
greatest of Israel's judges,

Men: O God of Solomon, the wisest of kings,

All: May our lives be but mirrors of your justice, lived out in the wisdom of unswerving faith.

Men: Great God of Lydia, seller of purple,

Women: Master of Paul, maker of tents,

All: Guide us into the world, unafraid to lend our hands, as well as our voices, to your service, and eager to involve ourselves with all of your children.

Women: And for the lives of all righteous women,

Men: And for past and present men of faith,

**All: For the ministries taking form within us,
and for all the callings yet to be:
The Lord's name be praised!
Amen.**

The Concluding Collect

For the concluding collect, the celebrant selects
- *a collect appropriate to the season or occasion being celebrated;*
- *a collect expressive of some special need in the life of the local congregation;*
- *a collect for the mission of the church;*
- *a general collect such as the following:*

1

Lord, hear the prayers of thy people; and what we have asked faithfully, grant that we may obtain effectually, to the glory of thy name; through Jesus Christ our Lord. Amen.

2

Heavenly Father, you have promised to hear what we ask in the name of your Son: Accept and fulfill our petitions, we pray, not as we ask in our ignorance, nor as we deserve in our sinfulness, but as you know and love us in your Son Jesus Christ our Lord. Amen.

3

Almighty and eternal God, ruler of all things in heaven and earth: Mercifully accept the prayers of your people, and strengthen us to do your will; through Jesus Christ our Lord. Amen.

4

Almighty God, to whom our needs are known before we ask, help us to ask only what accords with your will; and those good things which we dare not, or in our blindness cannot ask, grant us for the sake of your Son Jesus Christ our Lord. Amen.

5

O Lord our God, accept the fervent prayers of your people; in the multitude of your mercies, look with compassion upon us and all who turn to you for help; for you are gracious, O lover of souls, and to you we give glory, Father, Son, and Holy Spirit, now and for ever. Amen.

6

Lord Jesus Christ, you said to your apostles, "Peace I give to you; my own peace I leave with you:" Regard not our sins, but the faith of your church, and give to us the peace and unity of that heavenly city, where with the Father and the Holy Spirit, you live and reign, now and for ever. Amen.

7

Hasten, O Father, the coming of thy kingdom; and grant that we thy servants, who now live by faith, may with joy behold thy Son at his coming in glorious majesty; even Jesus Christ, our only mediator and advocate. Amen.

8

Almighty God, by your Holy Spirit you have made us one with your saints in heaven and on earth: Grant that in our earthly pilgrimage we may always be supported by this fellowship of love and prayer, and know ourselves to be surrounded by their witness to your power and mercy. We ask this for the sake of Jesus Christ, in whom all our intercessions are acceptable through the Spirit, and who lives and reigns for ever and ever. Amen.

Notes

Introduction

1 Thomas Merton, *Contemplative Prayer* (New York: Doubleday & Co., 1969), p. 37.

2 *Lutheran Book of Worship* (Minneapolis: Augsburg Publishing House and Philadelphia: Board of Publication, Lutheran Church in America, 1978), pp. 65, 85, 118. Hereafter referred to as *LBW*.

3 *Book of Common Prayer* (New York: The Seabury Press, 1979). Hereafter referred to as *BCP*.

Chapter 1
Praisemaking: Prayer in a Doxological Key

1 *Lutheran Book of Worship: Ministers Desk Edition* (Minneapolis: Augsburg Publishing House and Philadelphia: Board of Publication, Lutheran Church in America), p. 208. Hereafter referred to as *LBW: Minister's Edition.*

2 Henry Bettenson, *Documents of the Christian Church* (London: Oxford University Press, 1943), pp. 5-7.

3 This citation reflects the author's shaping of what is possibly a poetic or hymnic element in 1 Peter 1:3-5.

4 *Luther's Works*, vol. 8, Weimar edition, pp. 378-379, as cited in Vilmos Vajta, *Luther on Worship, An Interpretation* (Philadelphia: Muhlenberg Press, 1958), p. 14.

5 Walter Brueggemann, *The Message of the Psalms* (Minneapolis: Augsburg Publishing House, 1984), p. 15.

6 Dietrich Bonhoeffer, *Psalms: The Prayerbook of the Bible* (Minneapolis: Augsburg Publishing House, 1974), pp. 14-15.

7 Daniel Stevick, "Toward a Phenomenology of Praise" in Malcolm C. Burson, ed., *Worship Points the Way* (New York: The Seabury Press, 1981), p. 158.

8 See Brueggmann, *The Message of the Psalms*, Introduction, pp. 9-23.

9 *Ibid.*, pp. 11-12.

10 Dietrich Bonhoeffer, *Life Together* (New York: Harper and Row, 1954), pp. 48-49.

Chapter 2
Our Father: The Prayer That Forms Us

1 Since both titles "Our Father" and the "Lord's Prayer" have been revered in the history of Christian prayer, both will be used in this chapter.

2 Bonhoeffer, *Psalms: The Prayerbook of the Bible*, p. 11.

3 *Didache* 8.3.

4 See Joachim Jeremias, *The Lord's Prayer* (Philadelphia: Fortress Press, 1964), p. 17.

With a few changes, this wording represents Jeremias' proposal for the oldest wording of the Lord's Prayer. Rather than using his "Dear Father," I have chosen to keep the single word "Father" with "Abba" in parenthesis as a reminder that the oldest address was a single untranslatable word of endearment. I have followed the recent work of the International Consultation on English Texts in the use of pronouns in contemporary English as well as the terminology "time of trial" in place of the word "temptation." Finally, I have tried to avoid what has been translated "And forgive us our debts as we *also herewith* forgive our debtors." The use of the word "debts" is generally considered inferior to "sins" and the "also herewith" seems a bit cumbersome. Instead, I have tried to imply the causal relationship between being forgiven and forgiving with the simple conjunction "and."

5 *Ibid.*, pp. 19-20.

6 Ernst Lohmeyer, *"Our Father"* (New York: Harper and Row, 1965), p. 45.

7 Martin Luther, *The Small Catechism* (Minneapolis: Augsburg Publishing House and Philadelphia: Fortress Press, 1979), p. 17.

8 Lucien Deiss, *Springtime of the Liturgy* (Collegeville, Minn.: The Liturgical Press, 1979), p. 287.

9 Luther, *The Small Catechism*, p. 20.

10 Jeremias, *The Lord's Prayer*, p. 25.

11 Luther, *The Small Catechism*, p. 21.

12 Jeremias, *The Lord's Prayer*, pp. 31-32.

Chapter 3
Oratio Fidelium: The Prayer of the Faithful

1 Eric James, *The Roots of Liturgy* (London: Prism, 1962), p. 8.

2 John E. Burkhart, *Worship* (Philadelphia: The Westminster Press, 1982), pp. 38-39.

3 Peter Brunner, *Worship in the Name of Jesus* (St. Louis: Concordia, 1968), pp. 11-24.

4 Deiss, *Springtime of the Liturgy*, p. 75.

5 Marion Hatchett, *Commentary on the American Prayer Book* (New York: The Seabury Press, 1981), p. 89.

6 Deiss, *Springtime of the Liturgy*, pp. 150-153.

7 *Ibid.*, p. 151.

8 Theodore W. Jennings, Jr. *Life As Worship: Prayer and Praise In Jesus' Name* (Grand Rapids, Mich.: Eerdmans, 1982), p. 37.

9 J. Bonsirven, "Textes rabbiniques des deux premiers siecles chretiens (Rome, 1955), p. 2 as quoted in Deiss, *Springtime*, p. 9.

10 Deiss, *Springtime of the Liturgy*, p. 93.

11 *Ibid.*, p. 92.

12 *Ibid.*, pp. 82-85.

13 W. Jardine Grisbrooke, "Intercession at the Eucharist," *Studia Liturgica 4*, 1965, p. 147.

14 International Committee on English in the Liturgy (hereafter referred to as ICEL), *Documents on the Liturgy 1963-1979* (Collegeville, Minn.: The Liturgical Press, 1982), p. 596.

15 Theodor Klauser, *A Short History of the Western Liturgy* (Oxford: Oxford University Press, 1965), p. 49.

16 Grisbrooke, "Intercession at the Eucharist," p. 133.

17 *Ibid.*, p. 140.

18 Mystagogic Catechesis 5.8, cited in Michael Vasey, *Intercessions in Worship* (Bramcote, England: Grove Books, 1981), p. 8.

19 Luther Reed, *Lutheran Worship* (Philadelphia: Muhlenberg Press, 1947), p. 300.

20 John Cotton, "The Way of the Churches of Christ in New England" (London, 1645), pp. 66-67 as cited in Doug Adams, *Meeting House to Camp Meeting* (Austin, Texas: Sharing Co.,1981), p. 23.

Chapter 4
Intercession: Praying the World to God

1 Arbesmann, Daly, and Quain, trans., *Apologetical Works: Tertullian, Fathers of the Church*, vol. 10 (Washington, D.C.: Catholic University Press, 1950), p. 198.

2 *Luther's Works*, vol. 44 (Philadelphia: Fortress Press and St. Louis: Concordia, 1955), p. 65.

3 Don E. Saliers, *The Soul in Paraphrase* (New York: The Seabury Press, 1980), p. 114. Saliers has written insightfully about intercessory prayer in his book, *Worship and Spirituality* (Philadelphia: The Westminster Press, 1984), pp. 86-97.

4 *For All God's People: Ecumenical Prayer Cycle* (Geneva: World Council of Churches, 1978), p. 7.

5 ICEL, *Documents on the Liturgy*, p. 15. Quotation is from the "Constitution on the Liturgy" from Vatican II.

6 Eugene L. Brand, ed., "Northfield Statement on Worship" in *Worship Among Lutherans* (Geneva: The Lutheran World Federation, 1983), pp. 10, 11.

7 Hans Küng, *The Church*, trans. Ray and Rosaleen Ockenden (New York: Sheed and Ward, 1976), p. 389.

8 *Luther's Works*, vol. 35 (Philadelphia: Fortress Press and St. Louis: Concordia, 1955), p. 129.

9 "The Freedom of a Christian" in Bertram Lee Woolf, ed. & tr., *Reformation Writings of Martin Luther* (London: Lutterworth Press, 1952), p. 366.

10 J. A. T. Robinson, *Liturgy Coming to Life* (Philadelphia: The Westminster Press, 1960), pp. 62-63.

11 Goeffrey Wainwright, *Doxology* (New York: Oxford University Press, 1980), p. 71.

12 "Notes on the Liturgy" *LBW Ministers Edition*, p. 7.

13 *We Gather Together: Services of Public Worship* (Nashville: The United Methodist Publishing House, 1980), p. 7.

14 Louis Weil, "Liturgical Creativity," in a collection of essays by Mark Searle, *Parish: A Place for Worship* (Collegeville, Minn.: The Liturgical Press, 1981), pp. 85-87.

15 Lucien Deiss, *Springtime of the Liturgy*, p. 135.

16 Weil, "Liturgical Creativity," p. 88.

17 Daniel B. Stevick, *Language in Worship* (New York: The Seabury Press, 1970), p. 114.

Chapter 5
Guidelines: The Practice of Public Prayer

1 *LBW*, p. 65.

2 *Ibid.*

3 *Ibid.*, pp. 52-53.

4 See discussion in ICEL, *Documents*, pp. 596-597 and related references. See also *BCP*, p. 383 and the extensive discussion in Grisbrooke, "Intercession at the Eucharist," pp. 129-255.

5 Reed, *Lutheran Worship*, p. 256.

6 As cited in Stevick, *Language in Worship*, p. 117.

7 Ulrich S. Leupold, ed., *Luther's Works*, vol. 53 (Philadelphia: Fortress Press, 1965), p. 24.

8 *BCP*, p. 355.

9 Stevick, *Language in Worship*, p. 124.

10 Contemporary Worship 6: *The Church Year* (Minneapolis: Augsburg Publishing House, 1973), pp. 6-7.

11 *Occasional Services* (Minneapolis: Augsburg Publishing House, 1982), pp. 300-316.

12 *BCP*, p. 814-835. Additional collects can be found throughout the book.

13 Klauser, *A Short History of the Western Liturgy*, p. 41. See also the discussion in Stevick, *Language in Worship*, pp. 121-127.

14 Daniel B. Stevick, "The Language of Prayer," in *Worship* 52 no. 6 (November 1978), p. 546.

15 Nathan Mitchell, "Teaching Worship in Seminaries: A Response," in *Worship* 55 no. 4 (July 1981), p. 322.

16 *Occasional Services*, p. 76.

17 By the author for the Eighth General Convention of the American Lutheran Church, Washington National Cathedral, 1976.

18 *LBW*, p. 167.

19 Jeffery W. Rowthorn, *The Wideness of God's Mercy* (New York: The Seabury Press, 1985). This is a two volume set of litanies.

Appendix

Form A:
LBW, pp. 52-53.

Form B:
LBW: Ministers Edition, pp. 139-142.

Form C:
Richard Mazziotta, *We Pray to the Lord* (Notre Dame, Ave Maria Press, 1984), p. 20.

Form D:
BCP, pp. 383-385.

Form E:
BCP, pp. 385-387.

Form F:
BCP, p. 387.

Form G:
BCP, p. 388-389.

Form H:
BCP, pp. 389-391.

Form I:
BCP, pp. 392-393.

Form J:
LBW, pp. 148-151.

Form K:
Praise God: Common Prayer at Taize, tr. Emily Chisholm (Oxford: Oxford University Press, 1977) in Jeffrey Rowthorn, *The Wideness of God's Mercy* (New York: Seabury Press, 1985).

Form L:
Psalms 149 and 150 from *BCP.* Hymn stanzas by F. Pratt Green (Carol Stream, Illinois: Hope Publishing Company) in Rowthorn, *The Wideness of God's Mercy.*

Form M:
Lucien Deiss, *Come, Lord Jesus* (Chicago: World Library Publications, Inc., 1981) in Rowthorn, *The Wideness of God's Mercy.*

Form N:
Gail Anderson Ricciati in *Liturgy,* May 1970, in Rowthorn, *The Wideness of God's Mercy.*

Bibliography

Bonhoeffer, Dietrich. *Psalms: The Prayerbook of the Bible*. Minneapolis: Augsburg Publishing House, 1974.

Book of Common Prayer. New York: The Seabury Press, 1979.

Brand, Eugene L., ed. *Worship Among Lutherans*. Geneva: Lutheran World Federation, 1983.

Brueggemann, Walter. *The Message of the Psalms*. Minneapolis: Augsburg Publishing House, 1984.

Burkhart, John E. *Worship*. Philadelphia: The Westminster Press, 1982.

Jeremias, Joachim. *The Lord's Prayer*. Philadelphia: Fortress Press, 1964.

Klauser, Theodor. *A Short History of the Western Liturgy*. Oxford: Oxford University Press, 1965.

Lohmeyer, Ernst. *"Our Father."* New York: Harper and Row, 1965.

Lutheran Book of Worship. Minneapolis: Augsburg Publishing House and Philadelphia: Board of Publication, Lutheran Church in America, 1978.

Lutheran Book of Worship: Ministers Edition. Minneapolis: Augsburg Publishing House and Philadelphia: Board of Publication, Lutheran Church in America, 1978.

Ranshaw-Schmidt, Gail. *Christ in Sacred Speech*. Philadelphia: Fortress Press, 1986.

Rowthorn, Jeffery W. *The Wideness of God's Mercy*. New York: The Seabury Press, 1985.

Saliers, Don E. *The Soul in Paraphrase*. New York: The Seabury Press, 1980.

Stevick, Daniel B. *Language in Worship*. New York: The Seabury Press, 1970.

Vasey, Michael. *Intercessions in Worship*. Bramcote, England: Grove Books, 1981.